CW00548713

HOW TO [...] HIGHLY SU[...] PEOPLE + HOW TO RAISE AN ADULT + BRAIN TRAINING & MEMORY IMPROVEMENT –

3 in 1

Increase your Influence & Prepare your Kids for Success!

BY

James Goodchild

HOW TO RAISE HIGHLY SUCCESSFUL PEOPLE

Learn How Successful People Lead! How to Increase your Influence & Raise an Adult. How to Raise Boys, Break Free of the Overparenting Trap & Prepare Kids for Success

BY

James Goodchild

TABLE OF CONTENTS

COPYRIGHTS

The information provided here is correct and reliable, as any lack of attention or other means resulting from the misuse or use of the procedures, procedures, or instructions contained therein is the total, and absolute obligation of the user addressed.

The author is not obliged, directly or indirectly, to assume civil or civil liability for any restoration, damage, or loss resulting from the data collected here. The respective authors retain all copyrights not kept by the publisher.

The information contained herein is solely and universally available for information purposes. The data is presented without a warranty or promise of any kind.

The trademarks used are without approval, and the patent is issued without the trademark owner's permission or protection.

The logos and labels in this book are the property of the owners themselves and are not associated with this text.

CHAPTER 1: INTRODUCTION

Parenting specialists report on crucial facets of child-rearing, such as sleep, health, attachment, or training, but their guidance is usually narrow and prescriptive. We just do not need minimal knowledge as crucial as that about care and feeding for babies. What we need to learn more about how our children will be as successful as adults. We must also confront significant cultural changes in recent years — especially changes in technology and how these changes influence the relationship between our parents. How will the era of robotics and artificial intelligence work for our children? How's the digital revolution going to prosper? Parents globally know these anxieties.

As a young adult, I have taken some little advice, but I have chosen to trust myself for the most part. Maybe I was educated as a journalist or distrustful of my childhood authorities, but I was eager to discover the facts alone. I had my ideas about what children wanted, and I stuck to them, regardless of what other people think. In the minds of others, the outcome was, at best odd or strange. As if they were adults from day one, I talked to my girls. Naturally, most mothers turn to babies — a louder, more direct word speech. I don't. I trusted and confided in them. I never put them at risk, but neither did I stand in their way of life or taking the measured chance.

My philosophy was that I was trying to teach as soon as I could early in the first five years of zero to five. Above all, I wanted them to become confident children and driven, responsible people. I figured that they should face few problems because they could think about themselves and make rational decisions themselves. At the time, I had no idea that work would validate my choices. I pursued my intestines and principles, and I saw what served as an instructor in the classroom.

It's pretty strange to be a "popular" parent who has a magazine cover for your kids. I'm not aware of all the blame for their adult achievements, but all three were competent, loving, and willing men.

DETERMINATION, COOPERATION, AND COMPASSION

TRUST

We're in a worldwide crisis of faith. Parents are scared, and that frightens our kids – being who it is, taking chances, battling inequality. Confidence must begin with us. If we trust our parents, so we will expect our children to bring necessary and appropriate actions for empowerment and freedom.

RESPECT

Our children's sovereignty and independence are the most significant values we should give. It's our parental duty to cultivate the gift, no matter what it might be. Respect is a blessing, and it's a contribution to the community. It is the exact reverse to asking children who they should be, what profession they should be, and what their futures should look like.

INDEPENDENCE

Independence is based on a strong trust and respect foundation. Kids who learn to control themselves and to be accountable early in their lives are far more suited to face the struggles of their adulthood. Honestly, independent children can deal with challenges, failures, and boredom, all facets of life inevitable. And if things around you are in turmoil, you stay in control.

COOPERATION

Living together includes work as a family, at a school, or a job. Parents are expected to have their children engage in discussions, choices, and even discipline. When rule-following was one of the best talents in the 20th century, parents were tightly supervised. Dictating doesn't work much in the 21st century. Our children should not be asked what to do; instead, we will ask for their suggestions, work together, and find answers.

COMPASSION

It is odd but real that we prefer to treat people who are nearest to us without the courtesy and compassion that we give to others. Parents love their children, but they are so familiar with them, they still take pure goodness for granted. Yet, as a rule for the entire universe, they do not always know model goodness. Genuine compassion means appreciation and healing, loyalty to others, and an external view of the environment. It is essential to teach our children that the best and most exciting thing you can do is to better the life of someone else.

Our main aim is to build responsible individuals in an automated environment. That is what we do as parents, teachers, and managers — not only train children and run classrooms and management boardrooms but also lay the foundation for humanity's future. We grow human consciousness, and we do so more rapidly than ever before. You become your child's parent, and your child is the very being they become supposed to be with your faith and respect.

Within their babies, parents may create interest using similar approaches. They don't necessarily have to have the correct answers, but we do empower children to seek the right questions. We may say, "Let's find out if we don't know the solution. My grandson Noah often talks about the stars, planets, and the universe around him, complicated questions like "What are black holes? Do some work on Google, and we can go from there?" "And what does sound barrier mean? What does that mean?

How we are creating, whether we encourage creativity, is the imagination of a child. That takes me to the vision, a magnificently autonomous, curious by-product. Regrettably, our children are struggling when it comes to creativity and invention. In a report, a method was used to assess imagination and creative thinking in young children, based on NASA's innovation cycle. At age 5, 98% of children had a gift in creativity.

Nevertheless, at ten years of age, only 30% of children come in. Do you want to say how many people have retained their critical reasoning capabilities across our school system? It's just 2%.

You should do that as a mom, even if the imagination of your child isn't promoted in school: I used to place all kinds of furniture on a kitchen table for my girls. The posters, the colored paper, the books, Play-Doh, braiding yarn, and other handicrafts were given. They had to do what they wanted when they came home from college. I was also hunting for toys that could be assembled and built by them. The YouTube Kids App has interactive videos to make you learn about some sort of innovative idea.

Works such as these allow children to visualize and explore and, above all, play. Creativity comes from a sense of nature, and the child should be taught as one of the most specific items. A hint here: let it be. Without any help from you, they build their fantasy worlds. Think of a kid on the beach and all his fun games and adventures — collect cockroaches and shells, build sandcastles, skip bricks, jump on the waves. This activity makes them happy (and develops the right competencies).

The growing parent would like to raise healthy and productive babies.

Yet out there are so many parental tips.

What do you listen to them? When should you attend?

So what advice is reliable?

I have read hundreds of academic articles and research journals to address these questions.

A collection has been compiled of 25 scientific aspects in which children are trustworthy and well adjusted.

1. BECOME YOURSELF A HAPPY HUMAN

As explained in Raising Happiness, emotional issues in parents are linked with psychological problems in their children. Not just that, but even less successful parents are frustrated people.

When your parents gave you one wish, what will it be?

Their response?

It wasn't because they were spending more time with their friends. Nor was it that fewer would nag their parents at them, or allow them more independence. The wish of the children was to have their parents less stressed and tired.

2. AS MUCH WHEN YOU WOULD CELEBRATE WHEN A FAMILY

Happy families enjoy the things significant as well as small: a busy weekend, a strong education, the first school day, a celebration of work, holidays, and birthdays. The parties can be as easy as walking together to the park, or as complicated as a surprise party. Happy families contribute to more comfortable kids, so rejoice much as a family.

3. CONSIDER YOUR MARRIAGE PRIORITY OVER YOUR CHILDREN

Child-centered families have anxious, tired parents and demanding babies. Today, our parents are too strong for our children to risk their lives and marriages.

"A complete marriage is the best gift that you can give to your children."

4. GIVE UNDIVIDED ATTENTION TO YOUR CHILD

When you want your children to be healthy and productive, it is essential to communicate well with them. One compelling way to do so is when talking to you and give them your full attention. It is to lay down the newspapers and computer gadgets and listen to what they say. You will respond more cautiously, enabling the children to be more communicative.

5. SHARE MEALS WITH A PARTNER DAILY

In almost every region, children who frequently eat with their families will thrive.

These children have more significant language, greater flexibility, and higher grades. They are less inclined to alcohol, smoking, taking drugs, or psychology. And this is because these families always feed together!

6. TEACH THE KIDS HOW TO CONTROL THEIR EMOTIONS

Kids who can help control their feelings rely on results. That is crucial. Some kids are much stronger visually.

- You should express yourself.
- Sympathize with your children.
- Explain to your children that all thoughts are appropriate, but not all behaviors.
- Recognize the success of your children. Your children should be encouraged. To help your children control their emotions.

7. LEARN TO MAKE MEANINGFUL TIES WITH YOUR CHILDREN

For childhood development and psychological well-being, maintaining good relationships is essential. Kids who do not have such interactions fare worse at school are more likely to have law issues and medical disorders. How do parents do to promote positive relationships with their children?

Parents should adequately respond to the emotional signals of their children (see point 6). Your children would feel better by doing so. This action is the foundation of self-esteem. Parents should build a bonding atmosphere for their children as well as show them how to settle conflicts.

8. PLACE FAIR LIMITS FOR YOUR KIDS

Parents who set and implement realistic limits raise children with trust and achievement. Explain to their children the logic of the rules. These people set the values behind the rules that are set by these people. They develop a closer relationship with their children, in which they become more trusting Families who don't set limits: "children take the absence of laws as an indication they do not care for their welfare, and their families don't want this task of becoming a mom." Yet children require limitations to take advantage of their abilities.

9. MAKE SURE YOUR KIDS GET AMPLE SLEEP

Evidence suggests that kids who are sleeping have:

1] Reduced brain functions

2] Can't concentrate well

3] are more likely to get obese

4] are less imaginative

5] Can't control their emotions

Set up regular dormitories and that distracting behavior after dinner to help your child get enough sleep. Often, don't require screen time for 1-2 hours after bedtime. Blue light from electrical devices changes the rhythms of sleep and hinders the development of melatonin. To enhance sleep efficiency, you should keep your kids' sleep as calm and as dark as possible.

10.   CONCENTRATE ON THE METHOD, NOT THE ULTIMATE OUTCOME

Parents who over-accentuate success are more likely to raise children with developmental issues and unsafe behavior.

The way to concentrate on performance? Concentrate on this cycle. Children who are based – not on the expected result – on commitment and disposition wind up getting more results in the long run. See if you can appreciate the actual conduct, disposition, and commitment of your children. Naturally, they can produce better outcomes as time goes on.

11.   GIVE UP TIME TO PLAY WITH YOUR CHILDREN

I don't mean arcade or iPad games when I say "play." I'm dreaming, ideally outside, about unstructured playtime. For children's learning and development, how playtime is essential. The study indicates that the less unstructured children are, the more likely it is for their physical, cognitive, financial, and behavioral well-being to develop problems. A playful disposition is also related to higher academic achievement. Offer your children more unstructured time for playing, and they can develop.

12.   REDUCE SCREEN TIME FOR YOUR KIDS

The research cited to suggest a clear correlation between decreased satisfaction and less desire for Television. Good people watch less TV than sad people, in other words. A survey of over four thousand teens showed that those who had more TV would be more discouraged. For more TV exposure, this likelihood decreases.

Set an example by restricting your TV time for your son. You should also hold a private chat on the TV rules for your children.

(The study I found concentrated on Television, but with other screen time, I am confident the findings will still be similar.)

13.   ENCOURAGE THE CHILDREN TO KEEP A DIARY OF GRATITUDE

Maintaining a journal of appreciation will increase your gladness by 25% in just ten weeks.

I'm sure if the analysis lasted longer, the findings will be much more remarkable!

They had more optimism for the future, and they got ill less often. Not only were the people who had a happy, grateful report.

How do you continue to build a journal of gratitude?

Phase 1: Grab your notebook and a pen and put it on a table.

Stage 2: Write down two or three things you're grateful for every night before you go to sleep. (These issues are not concerned about how 'large' or 'small';

Here are a few samples of what could be written:

- Beautiful sunset
- Caring family
- Marvelous chicken stew for dinner
- Food traffic on your way home

14.   LET YOUR CHILDREN KNOW FOR THEMSELVES

The advantages of helping children organize their plans and set a report established their targets. For a fact, these children will be more diligent and concentrated and make better decisions. The study has observed that encouraging their children to pick their punishments is beneficial to parents. Children who do so often frequently violate the rules. Enable your children, as much as possible, to choose their activities. Twenty-four percent more often are students who take part in formal education because they want to go to kindergarten. Allow them the ability to make more decisions of their own as their children are older. As a result, they will be healthier and happier.

15.   SOLVE THE FAMILY PROBLEMS

Kids with extreme family conflict are more likely to have poor school outcomes, substance, and alcohol addiction, and mental difficulties, as Kelly

Musick revealed in this report. There are no surprises. I still connect with other parents through my job with children. I'm surprised by the number of families with big ongoing marriage problems among parents. This thing undoubtedly affects youngsters, who are less inspired, responsible, and dedicated. (Because of my findings, I believe that 30% of these relationships are split.)

16.   ENHANCE YOUR CHILDREN'S SERVICE AND KINDNESS

Kids who feel like something about their life are happy too. What makes them more attractive in their lives? When it affects other people, it affects their friends and families, for example, in the group even charitable, children are happier if they offer treatments to others than if they earn treatments. Ironically, kids are better if they provide benefits that they have instead of the same procedures that they don't have. To inspire your children, as a family, to support others and be charitable.

17.   ENCOURAGE A POSITIVE SELF IMAGE

The competent body image, although it can also affect boys, is particularly relevant for girls. One-third of 13-year-old girls are disturbed by their weight according to a survey undertaken by the Institute of Child Education. Furthermore, the Dove study has found that 69% of mothers speak against their children on their bodies. It influences the body's confidence in your children.

Anyways, in which the children should encourage a positive body image:

- Focus on the health effects of exercising and no more the impact it has on your looks.
- Focus more on the growth of your children's character and skills and less on their looks.
- For your children to exercising together as a family.
- Talk to your children about the media influences our view of our bodies.

18.   DON'T SCREAM AT THE KIDS

When your kids yell, your home will become a permanent battlefield quickly. Under such a violent climate, children continue to feel confused and nervous. Put yourself away from the situation as you are going to lose your patience. Take 10 minutes before talking to your child again to gather your thoughts, and using "emotion therapy," to empathize with your children's emotions. When it works, visualize a boss or partner in a room with you. And you're going to talk to the kids more softly.

19. LEARN YOUR CHILDREN TO FORGIVE

Forgiveness is an essential factor contributing to children's happiness. Mercilessness was also related to fear and depression. Kids who learn to forgive will create good thoughts towards the past. It increases your joy and your pleasure with your work. Have the children's role models. Don't condemn those who wrong you and take the opportunity to solve personal disputes. Speak to your children about the value of redemption, so that it is a habit.

20. LEARN TO THINK POSITIVE ABOUT YOUR CHILDREN

Entirely positive children seem to be healthier. How do you instill constructive thought for your kids? It is one way to motivate them to keep a log of thanks. Any other forms are described here:

- Take a healthy disposition,
- Don't whine,
- Don't argue,
- Don't make a big deal out about spilled drinks, split platelets, and so on.
- See what goes better for everyone and embrace it,
- Take your children into the optimistic expression, e.g., "I like playing David and Sarah" instead of "I hate to play for Tom."

21.   BUILD A MESSAGE OF FAMILY PURPOSE

Any company, including your family, will have a mission statement. This thing is an outstanding step-by-step guide to develop a mission statement for your children. My own family did this – it was an essential operation!

22.   FAMILY MEETINGS SHOULD BE ARRANGED REGULARLY

A 20-minute family lunch once a week would be suggested. During this conference, you posed these three questions to all family members:

1) What were your achievements over the last week?

2) Last week, what didn't you do so well?

3) In the next week, what are you going to focus on them?

My father held frequent gatherings when I was younger. Such collections brought together the family and reinforced the importance of connections between families. I still remember how nervous I was at these meetings to this day. So, if you haven't already, I urge you to begin this exercise.

23.   ASK YOUR CHILDREN ABOUT YOUR FAMILY HISTORY

Evidence shows that children who have a better sense of self-esteem than children who care about their family backgrounds. This behavior leads later in their life to their success and satisfaction.

"Did you remember any of your parents' diseases and accidents when they were younger? "And did you remember those issues that come to your mother or dad in school?". Sharing the past of your family reinforces family ties and makes your children more resilient.

24.   ESTABLISH   TRADITIONS   FOR FAMILY

Family traditions allow children to learn socially and to enhance family relations. Seek to build those traditions in your family with a conscience.

Several instances are as follows:

- Have breakfast every Saturday as a family
- Have a family boards game at evening games
- Cook dinner as a family
- Go for a walk at night
- Hold a weekly family meeting (see point 22)

25.   SUPPORT   THE   KIDS   FIND   A MENTOR

Kids who have a trustworthy person in their lives are 30 percent healthier than children who don't have a reliable relative.

WHY ARE RELATIONSHIPS BETWEEN YOUNG PEOPLE AND ADULTS IMPORTANT?

Many adults don't know how to work with teens and young adults efficiently and authentically, nor do they have clear experiences from the youth. Although adults can be moral, young people also report being disregarded or underutilized or worse. If young people contribute substantially to the strategy and execution of a meeting or conference, it will be of value to both ensuring that adults do not talk on behalf of young people. Adults and young people are significant assets of a country. It's a great responsibility for parents to grow their children in such a way that they will be able to do innovative things in the future. This responsibility is not only for themselves but also for their country. Young people need great attention from their parents. Adults have a mind with a bundle of thoughts and views. They seek guidance to draw their imaginative pictures onto a canvass. This thing only happens with the help of parents.

Sometimes adults become worse in their actions and make decisions. They are unable to make decisions on their own. At that time, they are dependent on their parents. And parents have to be very responsible in this case.

TIPS TO MAKE A YOUNG LEADER MORE EFFECTIVE

The core of this article is the personal experiences that I have in the form of advice as a young leader. It is for someone who wishes to become a seasoned chief or a senior one. I also have tips from close friends, leaders of their region.

TRUST, BUT BE CAREFUL NOT TO EQUATE CONFIDENCE WITH PRIDE

You will know what you are thinking about doing so. Speak with confidence as you talk.

MANAGEMENT'S VIEW

It's about offering something fresh or initial perspectives. Someone who knows and interprets life himself will separate himself from others. It means that you don't want anything off yourself. Try a specific description or interpretation also. You can never rely upon other expertise, job, or judgment to obtain that emotional distance and understanding.

INSPIRATIONAL ACTIONS

"Tell people to respond by demonstrating their determination and devotion to a better future. Make it easy if people want to support and join forces.

BE POSITIVE, BUT DO NOT AFRAID OF TAKING CHANCES

Is not afraid of being idealistic. If you lose, you must consider and change your abilities and weaknesses in the future. You will only optimize your ability by understanding your limit. Naturally, the breadth of the capacity will diminish with practice over time.

LET NOBODY SAY YOU THAT YOU CAN'T DO SOMETHING

If there's nothing, go and build it. Don't allow anyone to underestimate you in any situation. Usually, people never bear the success of others.

They always find a way to let you down in any circumstances. This is the time to show your power and to accept challenges.

BE WELL THOUGHT-OUT
You will need to be coordinated to function efficiently. You seem to miss those things if you're disorganized.

FRUITFUL THOUGHTS
Capable of entirely and accurately articulating your feelings and speech (i.e., communication abilities). It also ensures that you can assign responsibilities and express your goals.

YOU SHOULD SET YOUR GOALS AND STICK TO YOUR STRATEGY
"The easiest way to lead is often scheduled, schedules, and strategies. Usually, the flow is more powerful, take it as it comes, and pursue any new opportunity. Nonetheless, your goal will still keep in mind your final game.

"See for your reasons, patient. Go on the path of yourself.

BROAD VISION
Be sure you solve an issue with your programs, campaigns, and attempts and have explicitly

established what the problem is and how it is to be addressed.

KNOW YOUR VULNERABILITIES AND ABILITIES

Having a leader does not necessarily mean you are the brightest or most competent person at a party. It just means that you should coordinate people and use the abilities of each person. "The job of leadership is not straightforward — not everyone should. I believe you are not only a good leader, but there is no limit to what you will achieve if you are genuinely excited about your business. You can't slow down something important, and only your enthusiasm will move you.

BE IMPARTIAL

You have to be honest to win trust and admiration for your supporters. Do not look to your close friends or colleagues immediately if an opening occurs. Let us know and get the same opportunity, and everyone knows.

BE SMART

Seek an alternate approach if it doesn't work. If you don't have ample money, see how it can be quickly donated and loaned to you in your neighborhood. Be active and smart in any situation. Don't underestimate yourself and your capabilities. Believe in yourself more than others.

BE ENTHUSIASTIC

After all, hope is essential to improve the dynamics of this planet. "There appears to be what you think."

YOU'RE YOUNG, NOTE

Be robust! Be vigorous! I'm always trying not to be too bad. Recognize that you are still young and accept all the prime has to bring.

BONDING WITH OTHERS

You're never going to know if a human is useful. Via my family and peers, I built a support network. Everyone has an extensive network. If you want to communicate with a person you don't know, just enter and add a message.

THINK BEFORE SPEAK

Know when to talk, and when appropriate, give it. When a volunteer member of the team takes a mission or has a purpose assigned to him or her, they are committed to carrying it out. There are many valid explanations of why a person does not perform his / her duties, and if they do, you will embrace them. If I already have explained my goals or the inability to complete a mission (or have) affected the whole squad, I would not hesitate to be honest with everyone.

GET A MAN (OR WOMAN) ON THE RIGHT

It's a trustworthy guy. Surround yourself with the people who are credible and can work with them. Don't trust blindly on anyone. This habit sometimes leads to a significant loss.

KNOW HOW TO LISTEN TO SOMEONE AND HOW TO ONLY LISTEN TO YOURSELF

Try to prioritize yourself first. Listen to your heart. Develop the convincing power. It doesn't mean to listen to others. You must have to examine all the scenarios and circumstances and then pick a plan for a strategy.

CHAPTER 4: LOGIC BEHIND LEADING OF SUCCESSFUL PEOPLES

Many people question how they can excel and not know that they keep in them what they need to achieve their desired results. Productive people are today because of their customs. Behaviors at 95 percent dictate a person's conduct. Everything you are now and what you ever will be able to do depends on the consistency of your routines. You, too, can achieve happiness and lead a happier life by developing healthy habits and practicing positive behavior.

These seven effective ways of living are strong predictors.

The habits of successful people are:

- They are geared towards a target.
- They're powered by performance.
- They concentrate on practice.
- They're directed to men.
- They are well aware of hygiene.
- They are straightforward.
- They are autonomous.

For thousands of years, brilliant thinkers and theorists have been researching the quality of human life. For more than 30 years, I've been researching the subject myself. What I noticed was that the best people have healthy routines.

I've established seven helpful routines to build if you want to follow all you do to the fullest.

THEY ARE GEARED TOWARDS A TARGET

The first habit is to concentrate on the target. You ought to give yourself the typical target and to carry out simple, written priorities, creating everyday routines every day of life. The objectives are highly focused on these productive individuals. You know what you want, you write it down, you have outlined plans to fulfill that, and you revisit and reflect on your intentions every day.

THEY'RE POWERED BY PERFORMANCE

The second habit of productive individuals guides results.

This guide consists of two processes.

1) The first thing is to practice so that what you do is more comfortable.

2) Time control is the second method. This method ensures that you have particular goals on what you are doing and only concentrate on the most valuable use of your resources. Someone very successful is incredibly successful.

THEY CONCENTRATE ON PRACTICE

The 3rd significant practice you will build is constant operation. That is the most critical practice for material achievement. It's the desire to start to finish the job efficiently. You are capable of creating and sustaining a sense of urgency and a passion for action. Quick speed is essential about your success, whatever you do. You must resolve the delay, remove your doubts, and continue 100% for the accomplishment of your main aims. The blend of goal orientation, result orientation, and intervention orientation would guarantee almost complete results of themselves.

THEY'RE DIRECTED TO MEN

The fourth pattern is the attitude towards men. You place relationships at the core of your life.

This habit is your opportunity to practice tolerance, empathy, sensitivity, and understanding within yourself. Virtually everything about your life's success comes from the desire to get along with others. The good news is that, as you agree, you will become a wonderful person in your ties with others.

As Aristotle said, it is only by doing it daily that you can develop every behavior. The more in your interactions with people you practice being a perfect guy, the more you internalize these characteristics and eventually become that guy.

THEY ARE WELL AWARE OF HYGIENE
Health literacy is the fifth habit of extremely productive individuals. You would also keep an eye on your food and eat only the correct portion all the time. You will continuously workout, using every muscle and joint in your body continues to keep the body relaxed and fit. And finally, you need proper rest and leisure habits that help you to live your years in good condition in combination with diet and fitness. Note, your wellbeing is the only thing you have and is entirely dependent on the behaviors you build in terms of your way of life.

THEY ARE STRAIGHTFORWARD
Honesty is the sixth behavior. In the end, the character you create as you live is more relevant than almost anything.

Sincerity means that with everything you do, you follow the 'principle of truth.' To yourself and the world surrounding you, you are utterly impartial. You give yourself straightforward values and align yourself around your beliefs. You create your dream and then live your life in line with the highest ideals. For anyone or something, you never sacrifice your dignity or your peace of mind. This honest attitude is essential for your enjoyment of all your other good habits.

THEY ARE AUTONOMOUS

The seventh discipline, and that of self-discipline, is the only habit that assures others. The most valuable single attribute you will build as a human is your ability to discipline yourself, master yourself, and control yourself. The nature of self-discipline correlates with progress in every area of life. All these behaviors can be formed as priorities, outcomes, response, people-focused, people mindful of safety, truthful, and self-disciplined. Regardless of your habits, you are who and wherever you are doing. Since the time of your childhood, your patterns developed mainly by mistake.

Today, by making the decision right now to decide the pattern, you can fully influence how you develop your attitude and character and anything that happens to you in the future. So, you'll experience success together as you build the same healthy habits that other successful people do. Your life is going to be infinite.

You ought to be a follower of those who their dreams if you want to fulfill the goals of your life and to be incredibly popular. The more values that you possess, the more likely you are to excel. Successful people lead by setting some targets in their lives. Such people are very determined and punctual in their whole life. They set some rules to excel in life. Such people are the real heroes of the country.

HERE ARE SOME CRUCIAL POINTS; EVERY SUCCESSFUL MAN FOLLOWS:

DEFINITE GOAL, DREAM, AND PURPOSE

Successful people are still searching for meaning in general. You know what you want, and you have a vision about yourself. Ambiguous wishes and assumptions tend to unclear outcomes. This sense of purpose gives you the ability to stick to your goals and achieve your dreams.

KNOWLEDGE AND QUALITY

They are the best in their profession, irrespective of what they do. No research is too limited, and productive people are aiming for perfection. We are improving themselves and know that wealth is a by-product of their interest.

TARGETING

Successful people know how to work. You know that you can't do it all, so you concentrate on the activities which offer you the highest return on your goals. You don't believe in the multi-tasking myth, so you know the fastest way to finish your job is by completing something.

STRONG AND CONSISTENT DISPOSITION

Unique people have rational hope. Realistic as they behave and hopeful, as they think their success is imminent no matter what the outcome might be. They say they will take steps first, like a kid who is learning to walk, and then change their behaviors according to their input. This optimistic outlook helps them, if things are not done, to persevere and to be resilient.

VERSATILE
One misconception of the ordinary people is why they remain the course, regardless of what. This thing is only accurate if the purpose is still valid. Most influential individuals have done something different than what they wanted to do (Example: Steve Jobs started with machines, went to the animation, and made his comeback with the iPod). The future needs to evolve, and they learn even better today than before they began. It makes sense. Reasonable people know that there is no sense in continuing if their motives for doing what they are doing change.

EXPERT IN TIME MANAGEMENT
Successful people excel because they have learned a great deal. The best option is to make the most of the 24 hours available to us all. Extraordinary people respect their time and see the clear connection between the time and money they spend. Typically, the people who work with them are always on time and prepare to fulfill their deadlines by requesting rigorous schedules for their meetings.

STRONG COMMUNICATORS
People who can easily communicate are exceptional in their lives. Good communicators

understand that it doesn't mean they know each other only because people speak English (or their dominant language). That makes them successful is that they are transparent and receptive to their interaction outcomes and that they are agile to obtain findings of their contact methods. They are experts in the creation of partnerships and differentiate what is said from what is not mentioned.

BOLD & BRAVE

We've always heard the phrase, "No risk. No reward." but how many of us take the risk required to get the reward we want? Not many, but for those who do, they are the ones who make it and become famous. The good are bold to start AND have the confidence to move on. You are not only able to gamble but to go on your own. Unless it means going forward, they do not hesitate to torch bridges.

SUPPORTERS

Happy citizens are generous contributors. They know and are reassured of the "truth" that as long as you are honest in your gifts, the more you give. We work under the premise embodied by Zig Ziglar's quotation, "You'll get what you want in life if you support a lot of people to get what they want." The only thing you can offer is not money. You can provide time, know-how, money, etc.

STRONG SELF-ESTEEM NATURE
Unique people feel that they deserve their popularity and realize that they should do anything they want to do. You know that a mistake is what you do and not who you are. I also track the early signs of poor self-esteem to help retain a good self-image. They know that self-esteem is a state of mind, and it's much more critical for them to prefer to have high self-esteem than to have low self-esteem.

QUICK TO BEHAVE
We also hear of people who have the talent or who dream of a big game, but who do little. Those who waste their whole life, believing it will never succeed. Doors, not speakers, are productive men. Until they take steps, they do not consider the situation to be excellent. You just obey it, hear the input, and change your next move. Many in their lives who accomplish nothing appear to use 'Will,' 'Can' and 'should' a lot. Those that never get what they want are too late to justify themselves and reach their next objective. I advise you to find out some realistic ways to avoid procrastination.

CONFIDENT
It is what allows us to act effectively. Like chicken and egg, confidence will enable you to accomplish your goals, making you more optimistic. A great way to trust is to remember and conquer the fear of disappointment in the past. Trust means respecting others, not judging them individually,

and knowing that you still get the strongest and better the first time you do it. A mixture of confidence and integrity is a win.

GOOD READER

Many people want to learn, if not always, right. If you think that achievement is reflective and that you can achieve by thinking and behaving like a productive individual, reading will be an essential part of your everyday life. I have come to understand that it is vital for me to read books that make the most sense to you with access to more books than I can read in many lives. These are typical books that allow you to become a real authority on your passion or criticize your own restricting beliefs.

INTUITION OF TRUST

Those who excel in life have faith in their 'nice.' You do not explain why or how you acted rationally, but you knew it was the best thing to do. Successful individuals learn to use their subconscious influence by transmitting "words" from their conscious mind. This thing includes consciously visualizing the outcome in advance and then pulling in the details and evidence that would make the sub-conscious the materials for the execution of the submitted "files." Knowing how to meditate is also a perfect way for your intelligence to grow and communicate.

OPPORTUNITY TO LEARN AND WELCOME

Two people run a race and get to a massive wall that blocks their way. One individual sees the wall and tries to walk down to waste his time and wants to abandon the race before losing any more time. The other person thinks instantly about what the odds to get across the wall are. Is he/she going to mount, smash it, crawl under it? Whatever alternative you chose, you act on your decision and seek your input. No matter how you want. Good people have a positive approach, and they never hope they will learn about someone else. You integrate other people's aesthetic characteristics while at the same time, minimizing negative qualities.

ACCEPTANCE OF ONESELF

This acceptance was right to Polonius when he said: "To be true to yourself." Those who excel should not pretend that they are not anything. It allows them to share their imagination fully and not care about hiding who they are. The only way to consider one another is to respect others truly and to embrace them. You still just don't so much respect yourself because you choose to criticize others. The worst form of denial is self-rejection.

DREAM BIG

I've always got to read a wealthy person's biography but didn't have big ambitions to do it. Sir Richard Branson, Walt Disney, and Sam Walton were both huge dreams and accomplished much more than they expected. That is one of the reasons why they succeeded. You don't care about thinking big and go with it. Ask them about the visions if you want to know if someone is going to excel. They don't think big enough if they sound believable.

GENERALLY ROUNDED AND EQUILIBRATED
Those with outstanding achievements aspire to excel in every part of their lives. They lead a balanced life, become financially stable, cultivate positive relationships, improve their leadership skills, and accomplish their professional objectives. You know it won't help you improve your true potential by losing one primary field to another. You have to think about how you can pay the bill, and it is impossible to do your best to make donations.

OUTSTANDING NETWORK
Competent people understand why partnerships are critical and how they are one of the essential drivers to achieve your goals. It is also apparent to them that helping others first without receiving any benefit is the easiest way to create a secure network. Many that do not give up continuously create an extensive network very severely.

FASCINATING
The joy they have for their love and their lives is a sure indication of someone special. You are up in the morning as you know it will get you one step closer to your dream. Successful people

strive to be leaders as others are drawn to their passion and become supporters to do the same.

RECOGNIZES FAULTS
You should do two things to ensure you are not useful in the future: blaming others and apologize. You give up your duties and control while you do all of these things. You are merely implying that if anything goes wrong, then you accuse other people or making arguments. You have no control, and then problems happen to you, not because of you. Good people confess that they are mistaken so that they can work on the issue and not waste a scapegoat.

ABUNDANCE MENTALITY
Successful people should not treat satisfaction or success as a minimal way to deprive someone else satisfaction and achievement because you gain happiness and prosperity for yourself. You assume that there is plenty to go around and that it's more about profit-building than the competition. It is the attribute that makes them content with the achievements of other men. This mentality frequently supports other people's confidence.

WELL PERFORMED CHARACTER
Heroes are victorious men. Think of the heroes (films, novels, real-life) that you meet. Were they not both truthful and integral? Generally, they're not charitable and frugal with others? Do they not

just lookup? It is no different from being a hero who triumphs in creation.

GOOD COMPANY

As I grow up, I remember that through the business, they have a lot of knowledge you can know about anyone. Experience this idea when looking at people you meet and remembering with whom you share the most time. Some people claim that the average wage of a company is typically the five most people they get.

That is how people with conventional views prefer to stick together. It happens. When a group spends 65,000 US dollars a year, and everyone inside the company thinks it will gain 65,000 US dollars per hour, the people in the community would think it insane. However, the party of someone paying $65,000 an hour will estimate his religions in earning potential with the other person receiving $65,000 a year.

For you, what does this mean?

You are surrounded by people who live their life and pick up their values and their routines. It could mean spending less time with the outgrown men.

GOOD LISTENER

Many people want to be great writers, but not many people are willing to be good listeners. Listening to people excel in their lives because they can sense and appreciate other people's needs and spend their attention on fulfilling them. Listen carefully and ask questions, the best way to be an energetic conversationalist.

SELF-CHECKING
Good people never lose power. You don't scream or rage blindly. You have learned to control their impulses and are in a resourceful state knowingly (or subconsciously). You realize that you can't own or control what happens to other people so that you can change yourself and how you feel about it. Given how you think about it, another indicator of self-control is what you will be doing.

ALWAYS GET READY
Unique people are also set. They have Plan B and plan C, D, E, and F. They have Plan A. They rehearse the scenarios internally and imagine them visually to "think" what to do when the real situation happens.

CHOICE
People are in charge of who is right. You know you have a choice still. Their DNA, backgrounds, and circumstances do not make them victims, so they honestly do not feel the experience has decided the future. You write the story in life.

CONNECTING TO YOURSELF
Productive citizens trust each other. They don't have to be allowed to do what they want, because other people don't allow them to slow down by

depending on them. You trust in yourself, and your desire to fulfill your goals, whether or not anybody assists. Ironically enough, it is precisely this kind of mindset that encourages people to support you.

AWARE OF CAPACITY

Many who are great know that effective energy management is equally critical, if not more, than time management. Knowing that rest is so essential that practice is one of the vital crucial concepts in energy management. Successful individuals know that low energy outcomes are weak, and their need for quality is breached. Sleep your path to success is one of the better ways to manage your resources.

And where do you stand?

I think that you've verified several of your skills or generated action plans to improve the skills you lack. Use the ability to cultivate one or two at a time. When the values and behaviors of a competent individual are harmonized, you are shocked by how good you are.

START WITH A VISION

Before they buy the dream, people buy into the chief. —Maxwell, John.

A collection of goals helps to picture the real essence of management. Do not merely talk about an abstract picture but describe the objective with focused clarity. Remember the end goal time and over again to make sure you are committed to the finish.

Nevertheless, it is not enough to set goals. This thing is equally necessary to execute the aim and objective. Provide the team with a straightforward, practical course. Stay patient when it's impossible to trust in you. Neil Armstrong will not be the first man on the moon without the bold dream of John F Kennedy. Once you know it, no idea is too tall.

CHAT REGULARLY AND SIMPLY
Good leaders are almost always perfect simplifiers that can sever debate, dispute, and skepticism to give us an answer. —The correspondence from General Colin Powell is the primary connection between dream and fact. Lend the message of clear clarity and commitment at all corporate levels. The employees must understand why they work on a mission, what they can do, and where they should go. It means that they have excellent interpersonal skills, are a keen listener, and can solve problems. Efficient listening abilities are an influential leader.

DO NOT UNDERESTIMATE THE POSITIVE FORCE
Build a door if chance will not knock. – Milton Berle. – Milton Berle.

I had the opportunity a few years ago to invest in a Walt Disney leadership workshop. It was in

1928 in New York that Walt discovered that his supplier had recruited the bulk of Disney animators to launch a new studio. My best insight was this fantastic event. He lost nearly everything, including his staff, his jobs, his profits, and Oswald, Rabbit's hit hero. Then he gave his brother Roy a telegram reading, "Don't worry. Don't worry! Everything good. All right.

Optimism leads to the channeling of irrational anxiety and confusion into creativity. Skeptics will surround you as a dictator. Reject pessimism and transform constructive numbers.

ENCOURAGE AND INSPIRE
You become a leader because your acts inspire you to think more, learn more, do more, and grow more. — John Quincy Adams People build mediocre labor and get out of it quickly without the right stimuli. Some people are motivated by strength, opportunities, respect, and exciting jobs. This thing is up to you to recognize and inspire your workers with different motivational variables. You can also nourish the squad, which in effect, is a perfect source for success and commitment by taking care of them.

GREATLY WELCOME REVIEWS
Leadership and understanding each other are essential. —John F. — Kennedy. Kennedy One way to learn and develop is to embrace positive criticism gracefully. Many administrators, in particular CEOs, believe this "advised by their juniors" in their capacity is counterproductive.

Your people, however, hold the key to crucial knowledge that might help you excel. Leave behind your pride and wonder what else you can do.

MANAGED BY EXAMPLE
You don't drive people to find out and tell them where to go. You proceed to this position and make a statement. —Ken Kesey Forcibly, teaching and training are over. This thing is the foundation of future leaders through the talk. Seek to convince people not to lose time. Instead, prove your action the advantages of a clear decision. You can't afford for other people to do something you don't. You will set higher expectations and deliver more reliable performance in addition to gaining value and faith.

Thinking of your role model is the best way to proceed. What would you imitate? What are the characteristics of this person?

TAKE RESPONSIBILITY AND TAKE ACTION
A strong leader is a person who takes more than his share of credit and his share of the loan. — John Maxwell.

Don't tell anyone the blame. It is the least qualitative attribute any leader may provide. Working at the top ensures you own the dream and the decisions of the staff. Each company will have its share of slips and mistakes if they have a good range of internal controls. A great deal of bravery is required to justify mistakes and take action to correct them.

USING CONTROL TO SHIFT DRIVES

If the sea is calm, everybody will hold the helm. "Villain Cyrus."

Successful people never lose hope and temper in any situation. They are the boss of ourselves. Such people have the power to drive the ideas accordingly. As a dictator, you frequently face obstacles involving daring and different decisions. Confidently use your intuition to your benefit and authority. Progress is inevitable to establish a stable development environment.

GROW COMPOSURE

Patience and perseverance have a mystical impact when challenges vanish, and barriers dissolve – John Quincy Adams.

You recognize that a life cycle requires sprint times, followed by rest cycles. All of us are susceptible to prompt and pressurized decisions. Be cautious when excited and want fast results. Be careful. This thing refers in particular to small firms and entrepreneurs, where diligence will make or kill.

NO 'SINGLE' MANAGEMENT STYLE EXISTS

Swim with the latest in style matters; stand like a boulder in theory. —Thomas Jefferson.

How could a single way exist if there are no two people exactly in this word? Daniel Goleman researched over 3,000 mid-level executives, investigating six distinct types of leadership: order, revolutionary, associate, republican, and pacesetting. The engine behind these strategies is cognitive insight, which has a significant influence on an organization. While specific strategies have a more negative effect, they are ideal for other circumstances and individuals.

Both these cards are up for successful leaders who respond to the demands of their case. We are versatile and switch from one style to the next. To whom do you most identify? Prepare to relax and master the ones that are left behind.

WHY BECOME AN ADULT CHILDREN'S ROLE MODEL?

I remember how they became my role models when I spoke about my childhood. For, e.g., my mother settled a comfortable table, and with any holiday, she and my father would wrangle lonely stray. They encouraged me to try to be a kind hostess and something more. As I tried to combine motherhood and work, it was not easy. It took me too long to use the Wedgewood that I got for a wedding and packed it fast, that my 12-year-old child asked if the food was fresh.

I believe that any parent sees himself as a framework for the actions and beliefs of children. Yet children's worlds expand exponentially, and our impact is quickly diminished as a broader range of taste-makers have both positive and negative control—our impact declines per year. When children become adults, the sense that the sell-by date for character development has expired is quick to accept quitting the roles model business.

YOU SHOULD NEVER AVOID BEING A ROLE MODEL

The tragedy in parenting is that if you're good at it, you get killed! Your kid is off to college or the "real world" by the time you've finally discovered the fundamental realities regarding how best to discipline your child.

When you face a devastatingly complicated menu of parenting options, you'll have a specific but essential reality you can use to keep track of the wellbeing of your parenting style.

"If I'm hardworking, caring for my family, and leading a good life, my children would follow the path. See my point, are you seeing? The nature of the interaction is crucial to shaping people. On this point, there are tons of data.

However, one day, you will undergo an awkward awakening when you are as comfortable as being a good example. The purpose of my blog, like my psychologist for hundreds of parents and children, is to explain why.

LET US CONTINUE WITH WHAT I THINK IS A FUNDAMENTAL TYPE OF SUCCESS FOR PARENTS

The best hope of a healthy child is to have content + decent holidays + early schooling + children's internalization of the value system + spending Decent Time with children (QT).

Now I've purposely purchased them, and I know individual families are giving them. This is, it takes more effort and time to provide material items to the infant (it isn't a specified priority, though, it ends in this way). Some of you will GASP and say, "These men must be what horrible parents! "Well, think about this: How long is shopping or looking at the material stuff distracting you spend with your child? When you're honest, I bet more than you know.

I agree that we will spend a lot of time doing this, our kids need things. But it goes far beyond material need, and there is it they need. This thing takes me to the order I teach the hundreds of parents I served within Tucson and the entire country as an educator and clinical psychologist. How significant is my sequence?

They are helping children to adopt the framework of interest + investment of quality time with children + schooling + necessary supplies + quality holidays.

The critical task you have is to help your child internalize a set of beliefs that is their anchor on the rough seas of life. Here's the ticker: if you're not spending enough time with your kids, you probably won't internalize your value system. Any of your positive habits can be picked up, as they are genetically related to you, and science teaches us that genetics plays a part in who you are. Yet the world has a much more vital role to play. Parents do not spend enough quality time with their children. One of the most common and damaging mistakes I see parents make.

The specified quality time: we ignore our devices, our careers, our egos, and our personal needs and spend time with our kids daily, where we are talking to them more in-depth. We're laughing with them, and we're getting curious for them. We're rolling with them across the board. We should play with them in the doll room.

Of reality, we're doing within purpose what they want to do. If our five-year-old would like to ride a Ferrari to see what she can do on an open track, we may want to consider a different choice. Yet we take artistic interest in them, and we are pleased and curious about the benefits of our kids. We share their dream. Maybe we search on the internet for Ferrari's or go to the auto show for Ferrari, etc. And, we could draw photographs with this machine. It's just about us having fun QT with you. Parents will also show interest in the needs of our children and express them their dreams to be better parents. And we remain one of the fascinating people that our child knows through this QT we share.

We also internalize those ideals for which we have the strongest and dearest ties. You'll find that they are far more likely to listen and be like you by making your QT warm, entertaining, and enjoyable with your kids. You are most likely to come to you.

MOST PARENTS ARE OBLIVIOUS TO THE VALUE OF THE QT BEFORE THEIR PUBERTY

Warning! We don't want to waste too much time with you until they become a teenager. Yeah, they're going to come to you, just for cash and benefits more often. Yet you always want to see you, and when they feel pain, wounded, depressed, or confused, they will go to you for advice. The probability that these teenage years will come to you is strongly linked to how long you put in when you're younger. Your goal is to make a deep impression as a child so that regardless of how much he hates you (during such stormy times), he or she already considers you to be a person he or she cherished, respected, and admired. And think fascinating. So fascinating.

Sure, not always does your kid love you; you still have to admire you. The motivation that you will always have is profoundly tied to the degree. Which you feel you've been involved in who you are.

One of the most tragic things now that I see is that parents let their bond with their child be disrupted by technology. I noticed two teens seated at a table with their iPad at a Mother's Day diner. That was deplorable. But technology approaches and ruins the bond between the parent and the infant.

I know the parents lament when they come home from work, and I am a psychologist, therapists for babies, that they are too drained, so I sympathize with that. Nonetheless, the belief that partnerships are more relevant than something else, computers, the internet, etc. is ingrained in our family lives. One law we have in our house that whether the technology that messing with marriages, then for a long time, it will give the child a lift to help them to keep their devices from being so obsessed with them.

YOU SHOULD CONTINUE TO ASK QUESTIONS TO TEST YOUR CHILD'S HEALTH: HERE ARE QUESTIONS

Why are they saying they want you to be a part of the day if you told your boy what children want to do if they could do something for a day?

When someone told your child when it was the last time, he had QT when all external stimuli (including text) have been deleted, could they mention anything within the previous week? And in recent days? Can you list the top 5 interests/passions of your child right now? To what degree have you discussed and helped them develop and improve their bonds with them?

How did you determine how parented you were and how positive habits you wanted to adopt compared to what poor habits your parents needed to bring an end? Grandparents have the confidence to question each day, frankly. If you feel too angry, contact a source like a psychiatrist or a doctor who can help you work through that. Some specialists, such as myself, deal with emotionally dysfunctional parents or people who wish to change and develop their childhood. Just one or two meetings will make far-reaching changes!

How many routines (like meal times) do your family have to on a given day when all equipment disappears, and it is QT?

QT IS ALWAYS HARDER TO CUT OUT THAN SEEMS

A parent of five told me a day when her daughter read three books together, one of her favorite moments, and the mother then strokes her child's back before she rests. It may sound insignificant, but it's QT too. This caring mother does several things all at once: it encourages the child to learn how to read, to learn to shift quickly through a sleep period to help the child navigate the night with comfort and care. And the planet is balanced.

A FEW OF MY FAVORITE WORDS IS THAT YOU CAN'T BE A KID IF YOU WANT THEM

Some in becoming a kid may not realize that if you don't carve out QT frequently, you won't carve your kid QT for you as your child gets older. You're going to get sad when you grow older. You should carry it to the store. Even Facebook won't make you know like your kid is prepared to take the time to come and see you from their busy life for the adult. The goal of view of the adult. Teach your child that a strong, romantic friendship with someone else is one of the most valuable qualities. If you do, you're going to stop too many of the issues. This thing would allow an enhanced choice of partnership, better decisions of friendship, and better choices of alliances. You'll know what a healthy fellowship with another entails. You'll know whether or not someone indeed does. And you gave them a basic concept of how you feel to be genuinely and compassionately associated with others.

THE EASIEST WAY TO CONNECT WITH ADULT CHILDREN AND PARENTS

Some parents of underage children have trouble believing, isn't it? Or the parent still in diapers with multiple babies, right?

It's, but – rarely.

You have no control over their life after adult children leave the family. You don't "pop" them anymore. The only chance you have is to manipulate them. When they graduated from high school, the "raising" part was mostly completed. Or only though they have a license for their car. Parenting primarily affects you when they are away from you, and when they will do what they want to do while they are gone.

This is why early catching your heart is critical to maintaining your control. Even then, sometimes it lasts and sometimes it doesn't so you can do nothing if you're there. Your curiosity for them, your urge for support, or your feelings for them – thus often strength – does not decrease.

What will adult children's parents do, then?

Okay, I'm still very young, and I always hear about it. I got a lot of things I learned. I have even learned a couple of items from the many hours spent with adult kids' other parents – and their grandchildren. As a pastor, adult parents in our churches are an upcoming fight. I couldn't tell how much I've been seeing in adult children over the years of stress, resentment, pain, and even rage. I know a few young people who do talk, but who, by the way, that it was given to them, do not control their parents. I know that some of the parents of adult kids watching adult kids making wrong choices, so I don't know how to handle them.

Luckily, with my two adult daughters, I have a great friendship. Two of my closest friends, they are. Yet, I'm attentive. In their lives, I want to protect my power. And sometimes, I know the lines are sensitive. So, I reservedly deliver these reflections, realizing I don't know anything, but I have some "experienced" feelings. Mobiles and classrooms have made it affordable, convenient, and more immediate to exchange knowledge. Yet is it good for parents to retain a quick or continuous contact — in either mode of communication?

For parents, traditional modes of contact can be stressful. Most adult children don't respond to their mobile phones; they keep the voicemail boxes filled, so it is unlikely that you would leave a note. You will not read by recipients until you give them a warning text to read your post.

Nevertheless, as one study shows, after interaction with adult children, parental feeling varies; under various situations, it can be very uplifting or disturbing. For short, you can't get to your adult child with a mixed blessing.

WHY INTERACTION WITH ADULTS AFFECTS MOOD OF PARENTS?

The emotional best option for parents may not be to phone and fax are grown people, over the face to face contact. The study titling "The ties that bind: Midlife Parents' Everyday Experiences with Rising Children" revealed that 96% of the 247 sampled relatives with children aged over 18 talked to, written, or seen in close contact for one week, Karen Finger man from the University of Texas, Austin. There was regular interaction with a startling amount.

Yet, the scientists needed to ask interactions were influenced by the nature of the interaction between parent and infant, whether they had a significant impact on the parent's attitude and well-being.

A MULTI-REACTION BAG

'The optimistic and pessimistic everyday moods of the parents have been linked with fun and challenging encounters with grown children,' reported a study. Of the many parents who talked to their children during the study week. 88% talked on the telephone, and three-fourths were seen directly. "Almost all" subjects smiled or were discussed well.

However, over 50% had hostile encounters, including a "nervous infant" or a kid with fear about babies. Most parents had positive or negative interactions, and none had neutral interactions.

THE PERFECT PLACES TO CATCH UP WITH

The consistency of the relation between parent and child is essential; the extent and the type of communication depend on it. All three contact forms (telephone, email, in-person) were more likely to be used by parents who had more successful interactions with their adult children. Many with an overall good relationship about one and a half times wanted to see their children in person.

It is also notable that when interacting with children by telephone or text messaging, parents reported more negative relationship content. In the intimate touch parent-child in comparison, more negative partnerships were not dramatically related. One part of this research challenged the type of relationship most closely linked to parental issues. Investigators wondered if there were more parents worried about children in healthy relationships, for example, worrying about their health. The contrary has been found: "The infant of parents who had fewer supportive relationships is more likely to be traumatic.

GOOD CHATS HEAL NEGATIVE EXPERIENCES

A successful parent-infant relationship appeared to alleviate the detrimental consequences of a dysfunctional child, regardless of the adult child that triggered the original parent dysfunction on one day. The same boy or girl might be calling later that day to share a joke at work or an amusing story about how his baby sings the ABCs while asleep. The beautiful story will mitigate the trouble about the problem.

How do you talk to your adult kids? How much does this happen? Are your messages, texts, and emails ignored? Are meetings in person less disturbing than the online links?

CONTINUOUS PRAYER

Pray with adult children like nuts. For them, intercede. You don't have to remind them who you are – but I know who sometimes they would like to hear that really though they are not. Finally, motivate yourself until you continue to pray for them while you are inclined to think about them. This thing is more reliable and can be affected by one of the best forms.

SPEAK WITH RESERVATIONS

Should not express all your thoughts on how you can treat your life. It's their livelihood. In too many words, they cannot tell you, but even children in adulthood continue to live their life, much like you may like to stay in yours. You should share it on occasions, mainly when told if you think they are making a huge mistake, so if you share it, it's no noise in their lives. The irony is that when you add too much, "their" life again when they need it most, you decrease the influence of your voice.

BE A ROLE MODEL FOR THEM

Be the more experienced in the connection. It's important, right? You have more experience, and you're not expected to have more maturity? I had met parents who handle their adult children with silence when they didn't call when or work as planned. Was this the mature answer? How it plays, does it? It may be responsible for a response, but it does not encourage safety.

I know other people who use indirect coercion or place excessive pressure on their adult kids to call, to participate in other activities, or merely to respond to them in some way emotionally. Yet again, it can be the product of your skills in deception, yet it does not create a long, long-term, stable friendship that you ultimately desire for your children. (And that does not take care of it. You crave their love and wish for it).

Design the conduct you think to be that of your adult children. They are more likely than sentences to imitate actions.

KNOW THAT YOU WERE YOUNG ONCE

This thing is a secret. Recall what generation was like that. You want to learn. You've been dreaming. Perhaps you've been afraid and confused. I don't know what to do. You managed to put all of it for a few days. You understood it all not. You still have to know. You get angry occasionally at the parents. (Hopefully, you are still.) And you were made worse by those people. Recall? Attempt to understand them by recognizing you again at their age. When you can communicate for your period honestly, you will affect them more.

MAINTAIN THE DOOR OPEN

Be available to you as you put yourself at your side. When you lock the door, whether you draw sharp lines in the ground or when you make rigid guidelines about the relationship, it can be a lot easier to open the door again. (They roam even though we love Prodigal Son's tale because we love them too much!) You don't have to make them reap from you. You should set limits, in particular those that are in your house or for their more significant benefit. (This is not true love) (But remember that it's not your interests and for their excellent.) Any unnegotiable problems can occur, but let them be uncommon. You are seeking to build a long-term chance to affect them.

MOVING THEM RATHER THAN YOUR OWN LIFE

You cannot enjoy all the decisions you make. You might also think that they're wrong. Once, share your thoughts if there's an open door. I guess the easiest way to write a letter is even whenever contact is stressful. Yet again, it's not something you raise — you affect. So, they can accept your power, or they cannot. So, admire them more than you fear the choices they make in their lives, generously and unconditionally. And make sure they know that love is always unconditional. It will secure your power in the future — if not now. And in the days ahead, you should be pleased.

PROTECT THEIR HEART

Hold your heart and your life-particularly. Be mindful that, for years to come, you want the chance to think about their lives. Be here intentionally. Be careful to make decisions or do something that you can regret later on, or that will take you further. Do with your spirit – and yours as you do. Just like all those years you sought to shield your heart, you shielded your back. Ideally, you would have the opportunity to talk with their lives about their performance, disappointment, and knowledge as their power is secured as they can articulate their purpose.

And you bred them for this, recall. You have made your parents, you have made it into the world, you have taken chances, and you have brought it to yourself. They're just going to try like you did, and they're going to make mistakes as you did.

Don't fill up your mail before sending the recipient's e-mail address. How many e-mails you think were received by accident? None of me, but that's a lot of it. Don't be one of them. Don't be one of them. It could also have catastrophic consequences.

"The more you are, my easy rule. The more fruits you eat, you know, the more vegetables you consume. You know the healthy habits of everything. The more good habits you learn, the more good habits you become. (Unfortunately, that can be applied to bad habits too, so look out for yourself. It can seem all right to perpetuate a bad habit).

ATTENTION

It's all like the secret of everything. Hold your options and actions in mind. Don't be crazy for momentary or impulsive choices. There's a slight degree of spontaneity. This is fun. Not too much jumping through big decisions.

You love your brothers and sisters. And if you don't like them all the time. Once the end of the day comes, they're the ones for you. You're fortunate enough to have some good friends, but they somehow don't equate to family love. Do so until the day you leave this world, or I'll continuously haunt you.

Know that with all their hearts and souls, your parents love you. Perhaps once you have your babies, you'll understand this. This thing can sound incredible back then. After all, we didn't let you do much, and we haven't always been sweet or fun. We're still not that sweet or funny sometimes. Who thought it was one of the most challenging stuff to love you?

You also find the children to be self-extensions. Whether or not they are indigenous or imported, this is valid. Sometimes people say "blood denser than mud," but not necessarily enough that you can see Step-Dad's deep love for their foster daughter. You want the most for your children when it comes to parenting. That is why there is always no job worth losing the entire family life because it is a short jump to the next point. But how can you tell your kid what you have learned when you have your own business in order? A joyous and happy child is the vision of any parent. Establishing an infant is an act of conscience – no one accidentally succeeds. You may want your life to begin while trying to fulfill your goals, but how do you do it without paralyzing your children?

The iconic actor and martial artist Jackie Chan famously recommended that he give his hard-won fortune to his children as his inheritance precisely zero dollars. He claims the ultimate golden spoon is just going to hack them down in the long run – an audacious tactic. Have you ever wondered how to grow up a healthy and prosperous child? Any more, you will teach a healthy and happy kid. No more look here.

And if you chose not to do so yourself, it's real. Why do you build patterns without being a dictator in your children, so that they gain trust and achieve success?

I AM TAKING INTO ACCOUNT THE FOLLOWING OBSERVATIONS:

It's not easy to raise a kid. We always think as parents about what our children want, but never wonder what the children want. We believe that we know more than we do and therefore make correct choices. However, once we consider what they say carefully, we find that we just need to do something sometimes that children say. Every parent wants to raise children who are healthy and prosperous. Yet there's not much parental advice out there.

1. KEEP ON TOP OF IT

It may be weary, and often you find that the words go to and fro in one voice. But British researchers have found that parents with strong aspirations are more likely to have children. That grow up to be successful — and escape certain main pitfalls. 'a survey of 15.000 British girls around ten years of age, from 13-14 to 23-24 years of age, showed that those whose parents regularly had strong aspirations of their children were:

1) More likely to study at university.

2) Unlikely as teens to get pregnant.

3) Without a possibility of extended work periods.

4) Without a chance of being trapped in a dead-end, small-wage jobs.

ADMIRE THEM

Parents honor their children in two significant ways. The first comes because of their natural abilities. The second is because of their actions. For instance:

1) Lobbies for inherent skills: excellent work! You are so talented! You are so smart!

2) Lobbying effort: Excellent service! You've been living and finding out!

Low front line: thank children for their actions, not talents. You applaud them.

It is attributed to Carol Dweck, a psychology professor at Stanford University. Her dissertation focused on the teaching of the distinction between that disposition and a set disposition.

Yet when you thank me for my commitment, you encourage me to develop the muscles that you want me to build.

Consider again if you are a reasonably young parent and assume that this kind of difference is more necessary because your children are older. Only infants from 1 and 3 years of age will assess by the impact of these reward techniques.

LET THEM OUTSIDE FOR FUN

That one is easy. And it's entertaining for both children and you when the weather is good.

Consider this: all of us who work in workplaces continually told that we are murdered all day long. And then, for six or seven hours, what do we want our children to do? Sit back in the lectures. This is out of the mad maps. Science indicates that you can allow them as soon as possible to play outdoors.

"The more time children have spent their time lying down, and the less time they have spent on physical exercise, the fewer improvements they have made in reading over the two intervening years.

DO READ THEM CAREFULLY

This is particularly important when they are younger. Highly effective children's parents are those who taught their children while they were young. And the way is right, and the way to read them is incorrect. This turned out.

Only to learn is the wrong way. We were both (I plead guilty) here; occasionally, you teach your children so carefully that you're like autopilot. I may, at this stage, recite from memory the whole Ladybug Girl series of books.

But if you do, your child does participate more successfully in reading. Ask them to read book pieces. Tell them what the story would be like it. Tell them to change the pages for you if they're too young.

"If you were the baby boy, what would you do?" she wants to say. "The child can come up with another response that character can make, a different choice that character can make, even in books that you read 216 times together."

LET THEM PERFORM JOBS

It's a real item, I promise. Why do we, as young children, develop work ethics?

It's what you have: you make the meals, you mow the grass, take the garbage out, go to the house, clean our rooms — all the things children sometimes steal, and parents have to catch up for them.

"It is not just about me and what I need at this moment ... they know that I have to do the work of life, to be part of society." The downside as a parent is here now. Since asking a 9-year-old to fill it, you have always seen what the dishwasher looks like. Have you ever had to wash up after your 7-year old walked the dog with a bunch of plastic bags?

The argument is that it would be much simpler if you did yourself, especially in the early stages. The argument is: Yeah, that is not the case.

SUCCESS BECOME HAPPY

You are the world's first contact your child has and are a significant influence on him (allow me to use the men's word to identify both sexes). As Olukayode Alfred rightly said: "The first touch in a foreign country is most affected by you."

You are the first contact a child can have on the world and at home as a parent. A happier parent makes a joyful child; good children have the same thing. A successful child is likely to be affected by a successful adult. You are a tasty and healthy individual, the first step to raising a successful and happy child.

FAMILY TIME SHOULD BE MAXIMUM

You have to make time for the family alone to raise a good child. Your family wants time to express their feelings. It strengthens the family bond. Offer your family a time to feel at home, including babies. It is quicker for people to pitch ideas. You can fix challenges and raise mountains while you're with people who you're happy with – your kin. This is the basis for a healthy and happy child to grow.

FAMILY MEALS REGULARLY

There's an atmosphere that encircles meals. It's a happy glow. Make sure you have time to sit along with your mates. Make sure that you prepare the daily family meals. It's not a regular occurrence to be. During a week, there could only be three breakfasts and four meals. Cooked food is fantastic in the kitchen, and you can spend more time with your children. You can eat together as well.

CELEBRATE LITTLE ACHIEVEMENTS

A funhouse produces a glad baby. Families who celebrate their members' achievements continue to be healthier and happier. In contrast with homes where wins are not given priority, children from such homes appear to be more successful.

Promotion, decent marks, accomplishments, and other fantastic things are something you should enjoy. Just when it's the only party you can afford at this moment, you can celebrate with your family always.

PRUDENTLY SOLVES DISPUTES

You have to know that the state of your home impacts your child. Unresolved disputes never operate academically well for children from their families. Many of them have issues with their friends and men.

This generally leads to violence, alcoholism, and misuse of drugs, depression, and other social issues. Freeze it as long as possible if you have some tension in your house. Your child depends heavily on joy and achievement.

GIVE ATTENTION TO YOUR KID

The average four-year-old will be asking over 200 questions a day. Is it not that good to have an effect orally and nonverbally if the responses he or she gets were? The exchange of information between the groups involved is two-way communications.

Offer him your undivided attention while your kid is talking to you. It means having kind eyes and listening to him sincerely. You may need to lay down what you occasionally do at the moment. It makes him communicative and means that you listen carefully to him.

TEACH HOW TO MANAGE EMOTIONS

I think you need to know that any time I mention teaching, I mean – by behaving and not by words alone, introducing them to them. You would be able to concentrate more as your child is emotionally stable.

He won't get quickly carried aside or trapped in reckless decisions. The health of the body and mind is enhanced. Make sure your child understands all emotions, but not all actions, are appropriate. Empathize with your child, show for off, and appreciate the success of your child.

SENSIBLY LIMIT YOUR CHILDREN

In a law-abiding family, good children are brought up. We assign all and thugs to homes without laws or regulations that tie them on them (if we would call them apartments). The first part is: kids want to be free, but not to lose.

Children who are viewed with laissez-faire behaviors appear to become purple, and sometimes feel that parents don't matter. For the boy, that's terrible. The second part is that they should be small but not so choky.

The kid is in isolation or overstrained. It's dangerous. We appear to be too nervous when the first opportunity we get out of control. To raise a good and glad boy, set sound rules, and clarify the idea behind these rules to them. You will be caught by surprise as soon as he understands that the regulation applies.

GIVE TIME TO REST

Obesity, reduced brain function, and lower productivity are some of the effects of sleep loss. Based on the tasks carried out, there are various types of rest.

Take the time to rest for your child and regain energy. Be sure your child has ample time to get a decent night's sleep. Take the night rest to ensure that it is met with them. Limit the time of the screens and events late at night, which may disturb your sleep.

During your vacations, you can also make an afternoon snack. A peaceful mind is typically more successful, adding to a child's success and happiness.

ARRANGE PLAY TIME FOR YOUR KID
Some of the mistake's parents commit are that their children are not allowed to play. All works, no play, Jack makes a boring boy. You must encourage his child to play openly to make his child happy and successful.

Encourage him, not just video or indoor sports, to play outdoor games too. Although you can play Scrabble and other board games, you do need to ensure that he attends football or track meets. This ensures his physical and mental growth.

TV WATCHING TIME-LIMITED
Research has demonstrated, that the time spent in front of the Television and happiness have an opposite relationship. However, as in broadcast workers, there are a few exceptions.

Teens and adolescents are more likely to be anxious about that TV time. Be a good example and always restrict the exposure on television. Try to spend the day relaxing or chatting with your kids.

COURAGE YOUR CHILD TO READ

Someone of success has odd reading habits. Teach your kid yourself to read this. Per book your child reads successfully, maybe you add a bit of incentive. You can read a lot of books from your child's textbook to fiction, history, business, and work. Your child can read them.

Short stories are like a nutrient for the intellect, which stimulates thought growth and creativity. Take advantage of the right books and let your child grow into a good and healthy adult.

NOT THE END JUST FOCUS ON MEANS

Don't make the mistake of showing the results and forget about it. Make sure you show your kid how significant the outcome is. You will, therefore, encourage your child to keep up with the ideal outcome always.

This way, children gradually achieved more. Look out to consider the actions of your child even though you don't produce the intended outcome.

ENCOURAGE FORMING NEW RELATIONSHIP

Nobody will ever live alone. A partnership must be established. 'Show me your friends, and I will know who you are,' you are advised that you will decide your life with the sort of relationship you have.

Learn to develop a healthy relationship with your child. It will be to improve him and drive him to prosperity. For your child to develop friendships, you must construct an environment a spot to check your company with others.

YOUR KID WOULD BE ALTRUDIST
Productive people believe like their lives have a sense of self-worth – value for others. One way to do that is to teach altruism to your kids. Inspire a charitable boy. The period is one of the things for which they might be generous. Especially when they give of themselves freely, compassionate children are happier.

TEACH THEM TO SERVE OTHERS
Favor and support self-service orders. Enable your child to volunteer when the opportunities in the family, school, and community are available. Do not forget to carry your kid with you while you volunteer.

Give him space to support you, not only does it develop your abilities, but also increase your confidence. Encourage your child either as an adult or as a team or a family to support and benefit others.

YELLING IS PROHIBITED
There is virtually no excuse for raising your voice against a child who knows his right from wrong. Screaming also causes more problems than it can fix, so why do you scream first. Your pre-teen can lose confidence and become vulnerable to shouting. Screaming is a symptom of an abusive

home, and children from these homes are more likely to doubt themselves and feel distressed. You can always do so when teaching your child emotional balance.

If you are on the verge of tears, stop or leave the room until you are calm. Unless you should think about circumstances and come to a decision, do not yell to your recognized kid. You want a courageous, healthy, and successful kid, and you want to feel their frustration and let him know why you chose.

TEACH YOUR KID TO FORGIVE OTHERS

People who do not forgive are less likely to be satisfied. Unforgiven hinders real and sincere joy apart from alienating the human. Without redemption, it is unlikely for anyone to have a second chance. Don't take rancor and also don't let your kid carry rancor. Just make sure that you agree with the good ones by changing the incorrect ones. Forgiveness is typically fulfilled and less likely to experience anxiety and depression.

PROMOTE POSITIVE THINKING

Performance, happiness, and positivity go together. The truth is, no one with a good outlook will be happy. Have a good perspective, and let it be seen in you by your kids. Don't whine or take a minute to make a huge deal. Instead, maintain a good outlook and speak positively. Tell your kid the dark cloud's silver lining. They are hopeful and reflect on the bright side of events in this way.

ARRANGE GOOD CHILD MENTORS

As long as you see your boy, he still wants other hands to support him. In all but him, you can't be that. Help him and find a coach and support him. Trusted adults increase their odds of success in a child's life. Your coach can be a trusted friend, tutor, or a trustworthy member of the family.

ACCEPT YOUR CHILD'S MISTAKES

Luckily, in your life, your child can make no errors. Luckily, it's the ethic that your child wants to help develop. Which do you think is your child's healthiest way to grow? It's never going to be off and never have to make plan B.

And do you want them to benefit from and be open to errors? Growing up, being more educated, and making that experience as value? You would eventually restrict your independence if you were to choose the first choice. It is necessary to encourage your child to recognize errors. Provided they are still introduced, and never included in their narrative as the main statement. Overall, if they make a mistake, they will never lose, even if they forfeit. The healthiest thing you can tell them would be to smash the faults.

MOTIVATE THEM TO TRYING

The best musician, swimmer, or athlete, does not require your boy. At part-time jobs, they don't have to be the best. Yeah, at the age of 10, they don't have to train to write correctly. In the IFBB tournaments, they don't have to become Mr. Olympia or a successful star

But you have to do anything you're involved in and do your hardest. If you let them still realize this, the undue strain will be reduced, and they will be motivated to keep moving and succeed. They will not be burdened. Just safe should it be. It will also inspire you to invest in your hobbies and passions, for instance, if you choose to check out these top 15 latest NAMM 2019 items.

ALLOW THEM TO DO WHAT THEY WANT

Another thing is to follow in your footsteps, so to watch them do so can be very embarrassing. They will never be pressured to do so, though. You've got to create your reputation. We are enthusiastic about the future when you grant them permission to do so, which would be perfect if they want to adopt the motion. Otherwise, this is perfect too. It all depends on the point of view. You will undoubtedly grow a happy child first and a good second with these tips. Ironically, this improves the likelihood of achievement in your career.

Let me tell you that your child has a significant impact. Yet I'm not trying to do that because shaping is not something you should do now and not later. I also named the first argument, "The kid affects" You're already manipulating them, even though you're not sure of it. He knows from you through the actions of speaking to sleeping, how you communicate with people (including the child). That is why certain children are going to act like their parents.

THINGS CHILDREN WANT FROM PARENTS

1. Showing is more comfortable than asking me by seeing you when I am a kid. Give me a role model.
2. Send me kisses and embraces, loving me. With such, you can't trick me.
3. Child and strong discipline my brain continues to grow, and I learn gradually. Yet, I want to know if you teach me with wisdom and compassion.
4. Be still here for me, irrespective. Be my place of refuge.
5. Don't just talk to me.
6. Talk to me. Listen to myself occasionally, without judgment or copying, and I want to be understood.
7. Don't equate me to other children endlessly.
8. I'm going to practice a lot outdoors.
9. Give me a nutritious and cheap food. Give me milk.
10. Confidence, I let myself settle about issues not linked to protection or fitness. Without slipping, I could not learn to walk.

By taking bad choices, I can't try to make right decisions.

11. The support means so much to us.

As a mother of boys, you also understand their inherent distinctions from your children. Yet what do you do for these differences? Why do you discipline your children so that they are open, responsible men? According to Dr. James Dobson, author of Bringing up Boys, "the job is to turn [our] boys from untimely and transient boys into decent men, faithful and obedient to us, and secure in their patriotism.

We should also make the environment more child-friendly and particularly kindergarten. Most boys at the age of five (and some girls too) aren't able to sit down – their brain development is potentially dangerous. So, they are not able to know rote or have to read and write. They have to. They do much better in countries where children begin school at six or seven. Many youngsters, but particularly those active boys who have a good need for it, play and be busy.

This is only the beginning. The boyhood stages are not open to children. Another of which is the "full fours," which put puberty hormones well ahead as luteinizing hormones invade their bodies.

Four-year-old parents note elevated movement rates, rumbling, and disruption. It's a relief to know that it's not nonsense. (Although it is worth getting to the bottom of an abrupt shift in actions if there is anything bad). Yet it is prevalent for young boys (and some girls) to break out with excitement, and our job is to work out how they would do it – like they would have to do if we had a sheepdog in the room.

You should go up and wander about and have fun with lots of places. And help with learning how to put the brakes on a little soft but simple. When we make a child feel guilty because he is a child, we trigger insecurity about being loved, which usually comes out as frustration and a poor man's beginning. You should set boundaries and remind him to rest; please do it kindly.

Researchers in the Royal Children's Hospital, in a long-term survey of 1.200 children entering their twenties, found only last year another stage of infancy, called adrenarche. Adrenarche arrives at the age of 8 or 9. There is an increase in the number of hormones named adrenal hormones. I name this "emotional eight" because it's usefully presented. Your son is more likely to get frustrated or nervous or run abroad and is not generally his own. He's as puzzled as you are. Adrenarche is the initial puberty stirrings, but visible symptoms do not appear for three to four years.

More boys than girls end up bigger or heavier. Now that girls and women are so special, it is essential to teach them never to strike, injure, or insult or even rude. The emotional period mostly coincides with puberty, which mainly occurs two years longer than with kids, and when they hit full height and are entirely fertile (thankfully) is around fourteen. After 16 or 17, kids cannot grow in height or sophistication.

However, most boys are taller or heavier than girls, and consequently better than their friends. And it's utterly important to warn girls or women, from their mothers or sisters, never to beat them or even hurt them. Together, fathers and mother's ought to reiterate that message, stay with them, and recognize a decent man and wait and never go for anything else. Again, not strong or rough, just friendly, but clear crystal. To become a decent one, a child must know just what it entails (and, of course, see it done by the people with which he grows up).

Train your son when he is young to live the right way, and he can learn the best way to act and treat himself as he is older as he has been taught during his youth. We may not always be doing it "right" as parents, but each day we will try to do what we think to understand best about them.

THERE ARE SEVEN IMPORTANT PRINCIPLES FOR RAISING BOYS:

SHOULD KNOW ABOUT VALUES

How you teach your son influences your beliefs. Find the principles as the central foundation for all parental activities.

In any region, our values affect our parenting. Therefore, it is really important to learn about our beliefs. For starters, if you want to treat others as you wish, that will influence your child's teaching to respect others. Yet that would also influence how you train your child to take care of others because you first respect yourself, and anyone else is secondary.

A child encouraged to respect others as they do themselves is more likely to share their toys with their peers, and they realize they want to share them in this situation. Their peers are more eager to share their toys. A kid who is encouraged to think about himself first is less likely to share, as he has discovered that it is more important to get the toy than to share the toy because it is more valuable than others.

Learn your principles and your heart as you teach your child in essence. The following tips are helpful only if your child is trained to be a good, moral citizen with positive values. A structure of ethical principles and a sense of justice must govern their actions. It is the foundation for all the other abilities.

GIVE WAY TO THEIR POWER

Understand why your boys are more violent and thrilling than your girls are. Channel it into something positive instead of trying to suck their resources.

KNOW HOW TO REBOUND FROM DISAPPOINTMENT

Downfall's a life feature. Whether a man does not manage to excel will affect his capacity in the long term. When a man feels exhausted and cannot pick up and start again after a loss, he will never be through. As men are encouraged to gather and try again during their youth, they learn how to get out of defeat.

It is a good lesson to tell your son to try again after defeat. It can be achieved by highlighting the commitment and not the result.

For starters, you would drop several times before your child learns his talent if you teach your son to ride a bike. You inspire them to get up and do something over and again. Do not emphasize the outcome, which runs on a two-wheel bike alone. Rather, thank them as they have worked hard and stood up and tried it again. They will finally learn to cycle successfully after an ample attempt. You should certainly compliment them as they have the potential to learn, but once again, make sure to emphasize their hard work and perseverance until they have succeeded.

Time, commitment, and energy are required to succeed. The easiest way for your child to develop a mindset that produces results is to increase concern over the result.

When you rely on the result, for example, winning a game, when you have a failure, you feel defeated.

We are now likely to see where we could change if they can go through the game and appreciate their hard work and their positive efforts. It's going to make them stand up and start again, so they don't look like an utter disaster. You can see the benefit of their good work and a mentality that can start again, and that can be changed.

CARE FOR THEIR ESSENCE

Understand that in this world, many scary things can harm the heart of your people. Dobson recommends that "the threats must be aggressively treated, exposure to public abuse minimized and symptoms of distress, kidnapping or lethargy are detected."

TRY TO KEEP THEM NEAR TO YOU

Hold your sons in close touch. Maintain free contact, direction, and discipline by devotion. Kids tend to be with their kin. I like both mom and dad for quality time and quantity.

Many conditions are not sustainable, in particular considering the rise in single motherhood levels. Studies have shown that single mothers raise boys well, provided they have a good role model for children. The next best thing if the dad cannot be in the picture is a decent father, who will affect the child's life positively.

According to the National Economics Editorial, single motherhood in the U.S. is around 40%. When contrast with children in typical families in which both a mother and rear father, children with single mothers have significantly lower moral test expectations and are more violent.

However, for single mothers, all hope is not lost. Our everyday life's work found that having the presence of a parent or grandmother in a child's life would help the child boost his or her educational results. They are less likely to be arrested, less likely to experience substance addiction, and may experience greater confidence and good self-esteem. This helps young people tremendously. They are not to be taken lightly. Our children need good male role models, and if possible, a father in their lives, to help them grow and succeed.

When a dad isn't in the picture, instead, the void can be filled by a brother, uncle, or family member. Good role models are important as they form the way life can be carried out. Kids deserve to spend time with a parent, or a strong male role figure, to figure and tutor, and to encourage them to be decent guys.

BE A ROLE MODEL FOR THEM

Provide good role models for your children. When your dad's not at home, try sharing time with a close family member or relative.

GIVE YOUR TIME PROPERLY

Give your children plenty of time with each other. You may need to change your timetable, but give your children time and content. People think that a boy can become vulnerable with a hug or love. This just doesn't happen. We show them how to kiss and "I love you" is behavior that makes them better boyfriends, wives, mothers, and role models as adults. It also gives you tremendous benefits, including physical well-being, lowered anxiety, enhanced coordination, increased gladness, and decreased health-line tension.

Some therapists prescribe a minimum of 12 snacks a day for progress, and others suggest as many snacks as we can and offer better outcomes on a regular basis.

Everything wants attention and affection. Hugging is a primary means for parents to have a happy, supportive every day for our children. Depending on their home experiences, our children tend to be affectionate. If you grew up in a family that has never earned a cuddle, you would possibly find it uncomfortable as an adult. Inform her that affection is good and let her take advantage of those kisses every day. Use it as a habit to embrace your son regularly and say, 'I love you.' The benefits are, therefore, important to you.

SUPPORT THEIR NEEDS

"Counteract the impact of man-bashing in our society by the reinforcement of the manhood and the importance of a boy as a human."

Kids will have visions. Dreamless life is a dreamless life. Don't pinch your hopes by crushing them before they can attempt to follow them.

Your child may want as an adult, for instance, to be a professional footballer. Hope and vision were theirs. They're 14, and that's their desire to survive now. Many parents have decided to make those visions seem impossible. The prospects of becoming a professional athlete like a footballer will be slim, but they should not be trying. They must learn over time that they are truly strong enough to leap to the next stage by their involvement in the sport.

That's why having your child be well-rounded is vital. As the old saying goes, you cannot put all the eggs in a single basket. Rather, the value of other activities should be learned, and the school will work hard, and you never know whether the accident will actually keep you out of a sport. And if it sounds like one in a million shots a kid follows their dreams, they are given important life lessons. You know how to work hard, and you figure out what it takes to be the best thing you dream of.

Nothing positive happens easily in practice. If this is their dream, then let them do it (not to sell your house to finance the rocket development project). Enable them to earn the rocket fuel. We will see what it takes to get there like that.

If you don't reach that goal, it's all right, too. It is interesting to hear what they have learned along the way. We heard about teamwork, physical fitness, planning, and dedication, for example, as a football player. It wasn't anything at all. They will never become a pro soccer player, but over time, they may discover the truth.

A parent wants no truth to break illusions. Enable children to hope and to dream, for this is what makes them do their hardest to make every effort.

The opportunities to work hard even with disappointment are good things to learn from experience. Don't discourage them from chasing a vision because they are scared that they will embarrass themselves. Failure and the desire to get up after a defeat ensures that they are powerful guys.

A RELIGION NURTURE

Make the spiritual growth of your children your first priority in parental education by encouraging them to establish their relationship with God.

TRAIN TO PLAY A STRONG PERSON

A good sport is a key learning capability. In practice, we can't compete. Everyone will ultimately fail. Parents should teach this ability to their young children.

For starters, when you play a board game, and your brother loses, you should not sulk but congratulate your brother. When you have played, have you told them verbally "friendliness, good game." Starting young is a healthy idea. When they've been able to meet other champions along the road, it will make it more enjoyable to be a good athlete as a teen or an adult. Stanford Children's Health described healthy sports as:

Good sport can seem impossible to decide, but its defining characteristics include being able to win, value one's rivals, and lose with grace.

TO BUILD A STRONG ETHICS JOB

Do not do everything for them! Do not do everything for them. Try to train your kids to work with a strong work ethic. Although mum does it for them every day, they won't learn to make their bunk. Via everyday practice, they learn accountability and positive professional ethics.

It should begin at a young age. Once the kid is three years old, he can assist with the necessary household activities like recycling garbage, gathering toys, feeding animals, and washing. You may not do the best job at all, but you begin to educate you when you are young. Provide them frequently with critical life and family knowledge through education. This allows you to build a strong ethic at work. You will grow up and know that you can throw out the garbage until it is complete, as you have done it for years before you reach maturity.

Don't presume why other household tasks belong to boys and others to girls. Teach all girls and boys all their skills through activities. Sons must be taught cooking, sweeping, and washing. What would do things for them as they leave home and go to college or their first job? You must learn these skills to do better for yourself.

This makes them both a great, preferred 9partner and husband. No woman wants to marry a man who can't do household work. You may fault your parents for not educating you, but if you do not know how to commit to homework, it will not help you get a better partner.

Having a successful girlfriend, husband, and wife means having able to do things like washing and cooking, and having washing, heating, and all the homework. This is not a healthy way of educating others for themselves, or train them for any partnership in the future, to ask others to do so when their moms did as they grew up. When you would ever like to stay alone, outside your home, teach them sound work ethics, it ends with household duties.

TEACH STRONG QUALITIES IN CONVERSATION

Communication skills are essential for any child's relationships and professions to be productive. The foundations for human contact are communication skills. If they find it difficult to connect, relationships and career goals can become more challenging to achieve. Livestrong.com notes that technology is a big reason for the lack of effective listening skills for many youngsters. In an environment of pervasive email and instant messaging, their face-to-face encounters are impaired. So much time is spent outside of positive face-to-face experiences. The very first step in establishing effective communication skills is to limit your child's exposure to technology and resources. Speak to your child every day, and chat is useful in developing positive communication skills.

If you already have a teen who has trouble acquiring strong qualities in speech. Not too late.

Not too late. We can also learn these skills, but during our lives, we can still develop more vital communication skills. One approach to teens is by sports. Good contact. Strong listening ability can be learned by chatting, form these skills, and open-ended questions for those of those with younger people.

This involves laughing, complimenting, posing questions, and responding kindly to justify their guidance. This method of speech, both verbal and nonverbal, is an excellent means of educating children and can help children build friendships both now and in the future.

FREQUENTLY INDULGE IN POLITICAL AND MANNER LECTURES

It is not a one-time lesson to teach your son good ways. It's a daily childhood lesson. Take time every day in your house to use and apply proper etiquette and politeness. It is how you can help your son become a respectful man. It means you can show them how to eat socially from the moment they prepare to sit at a dining table. We should try to eat with their mouths closed on the dining table, and use the best silverware, no cocks on the table. If you don't learn to exercise those things at home, you won't develop the things via natural means.

In relationships, courtesy is significant, but also on the front of the job. Study.com demonstrates that you should train for career advancement and referral letters in an appropriate style. For example, if you tell your son that he can be respectful and accommodating to others, even though they are not especially good to him, that will help him learn how to interact in the future with rough co-workers. In his life, your son still is going to have rough men. Finding good ways to treat them is important to his life's progress.

ENABLE HIM TO GROW HIS CHILD'S HEART AND DESIRE FOR SUPPORT

To our girls, compassion is something that we all will like. Your generosity to others will affect their environment. Not just your relationship with your future wife, but also your future children, your coworkers, and your friends.

Teaching our children to be kind makes them change the environment. Some realistic ways to make your child kind are available:

- Model compassion
- Teach the principle that you treat someone as you expect them to love
- Take them on volunteer service to and serve someone (when you are compassionate in your heart and positive in mind)
- Teach them to express words of appreciation and sincere gratitude towards others
- Lead them never to be a tyrant
- Teach them to treat people with respect, because it does make them behave in the right manner, it is nice

- Model appreciation
- Teach children to be thankful for their lives and situations

CREATING SKILLS INSTILLING PEER OPPOSITION DETERMINATION

Parental pressure is actual. Pair competition is a reality. This starts when young and does not end in adulthood. We must teach our babies, even though their peers seek to bring pressure on them in other decisions, to make good and stand up for these decisions.

Skills You Need explains ways in which we should teach our children to peer resistance. It involves training them first on how to recognize their correct judgment in these conditions of social pressure, how to speak up for their opinions and beliefs, and eventually to show them how to express their stance assertively.

You can help them to practice their defense of themselves and their decisions by playing scenarios with your child. You may play a part, for example, where your child receives nice medicines. Practice them first by asking you that they want to say 'no' to drugs because they have to trust in the decision. Help them then to find belief in their belief so that they have a firm basis for their decision. When they don't think they want to, their only excuse might not be adequate because it is their closest friend who guarantees the closest they will ever meet. Enable them to realize their beliefs and why they say no to drugs, or whatever the scenario you watch.

Then advise them to respond no strongly. In that case, for example, it may be because they are learning ways to express it in their terms which is relaxed but firm, such as "no, I'm not taking drugs, and I'm not going to lose my right to attend college for the failure of a drug check or being caught doing the drugs."

Teach your child by justifying their positive choices to avoid social pressure. If you know any of his buddies had a disabled kid on the playground, but he was sticking up for the boy, then pick up his wife! Let him think that it is smart decision-making to do things better and not to do as his friends did.

We need to learn where they are in critical problems to be peer-resistant. The next tip is also quite necessary.

EXPLAIN TO THEM THE IMPORTANCE OF HEALTHY LIVES

If they learn right from wrong, they can't make good life decisions for your kids. This lesson ends in the building. If you want to improve your son, encourage him to make positive decisions for his future, including no drugs, alcohol, underage drinking, and pornography because it is seen as extraordinarily addictive and counteractive to healthy growth. Which are not the only forms of drug avoidance vices of parents?

While alcohol and drugs seem to be the most prevalent stimulants in adolescents, illnesses such as videogames, gambling, sexuality, shopping, or the Internet cause other addictions, any excess which affects the ability to work on a daily basis regularly should be dealt with. Some of these problems should be avoided, for example, to discourage game abuse and not to grant your sons available free time. Have set daily gambling time limits and technology access. Have your son interested in fun gaming events so that he doesn't just concentrate every day on his time in the game. Support him to pursue these other things, and he wants hobbies and passions beyond gaming.

Discuss with your child the choices they make for their lives and how their choices will impact their future. For starters, a teen might feel that smoking marijuana often isn't essential. One may be unaware of the zero tolerance of the narcotics program, even the marijuana, at the institution they plan to attend. Often, the dangers and drawbacks of smoking pots for teenagers may not be understood. Address the main problems and even the minor ones. Before taking bad calls, have the tough talks.

A parent gives a list of supportive ways in which parents can assist their children in making wise decisions. Help them see the consequences of their choices, even minor ones. You should not believe your child's science experiment, for example. We are the only ones who will not get an exhibit on the day of the science fair. You didn't call for your help. It was probably because of suggesting to you that they had a job to be completed before the day before. Their choices have consequences, and guardians must encourage their children to understand that their actions and preferences have a personal impact.

If a mother feels sorry for her son because her science experiment isn't finished, so she whips something for him when he sleeps the night before it leaves, then the son learns because his mother will save him as things get rough. He won't feel the regret that he hasn't had a job and can't attend the technology trade fair. Since mom fixes problems, he won't get a poor score.

Over the long term, it doesn't help him. He must undergo these shortcomings in order to grasp the consequences of his acts and decisions. If a project does not finish, it will lead to failure, and in the specified amount of time, he made the conscious decision not to do the job.

HONESTY IS THE BEST POLICY

Adult dishonest and deceiving people have an evil heart. When you want to make your son a man of honor, so from a young age, they have to understand that honesty is incredibly necessary. Below are a few ways that your child should be frank.

1) Honesty Template.

2) Do not say white lies because kids still cannot distinguish between small lies and significant lies.

Do not fib at all, because you are their only truth-telling role model.

3) Promote sincerity: When you believe you should be disciplined for telling the truth, you won't be told.

4) Giving your child a chance, without pushing him, to tell the truth.

5) Should not commit children's lying to make your life simpler. Of starters, it makes you a thief to convince them that the park is closed and you can't go there today. Do not even lie to your kid for a better or more obedient life. Be blunt. For example, when you don't have time to take them to the park, then you can't go to the park today, but two days later you'll take them there and as you've agreed.

6) On your word, please be good. If you say something, do it. This makes you cheat because you don't follow through.

7) Don't be accusatory because you ask your child to know the truth about a case. When you are, for example, suspecting that a lamp hit your son in your living room, don't run to him shouting: "I think you've hit a lamp, best tell me what you're doing right now." Forcing an honest answer out of coercion doesn't encourage him to be honest. This tells only when the truth gets him into trouble, to cover the facts.

8) When you confess to lying, think to the victims and about how their mistakes and relations have

hurt. Enable them to see that relationships are detrimental and deception.

9) Praise your child for having said the truth, particularly when it may be hard to tell the truth.

SUPPORT HIM FIGURE OUT HIS STRENGTHS AND INTERESTS

When you're not serious about what you are doing, it is impossible to excel. For our children, that's the same thing. We have to discover what our children are passionate about in life if we want to succeed. The easiest way to attain achievement and joy is to learn what they are good at, their talent, and where their interests intersect.

Parents must be careful to identify the skills and natural capabilities of their sons. Then, if your son loves doing anything, give them a chance to discover and develop their ability into an exercise. If you see your child getting a strong synchronization of hand and eye with a goal, you may want to engage him in a soccer season, for example, and you love tossing a goal in your backyard at night. This will become a hobby if he retains a skill and loves the sport.

Learning to develop a skill with enthusiastic determination is a major skill that allows them to excel in their lives. It's difficult to be excited when you work hard if you're never passionate about anything. They'll discover their willingness to search deeply and work hard where they find love. This allows us in the long term to establish positive work ethics. As people, it would make them glade.

You, as a mom, should help your child experience things and experiences that make him passionate about his life at a young age, so that he or she can find ways and opportunities to improve his / her talents to make this desire for a cause work.

TEACH HEALTHY HABITS FOR RISING

People with inadequate treatment can have trouble with relationships and work. If they are interviewed in a warped costume, poor breath, and body scent, they advise the interviewing person that the role is not sufficiently necessary to try to look and smell good.

It's an ability that all boys should be taught is essential to dress nice and clean. You will know how to use iron and how to fit clothing correctly. Boys should know what proper grooming and cleaning practices mean from an early age as well.

Parents need to teach their kids how to comb their hair every day, how to trim their nails, shower daily, clean their teeth, change clothes, and frequently shower or bathe. Many boys are avoiding proper grooming and taking care of their bodies during periods. It is where parents will participate and set specific grooming standards. For example, if your son fails to shower and you rule to shower every other day, and it was a week now, then you will forfeit all social rights and technology, for instance, before they shower.

In training them, you know how to look after your bodies. Good grooming practices can be a routine that starts as soon as you can clean your own teeth. We don't know how osmosis can do these things. We need to be shown how proper grooming and personal care feel.

Both conditions can be resolved and avoided in certain ways, including stinky shoes, body order, and greasy hair. Decent people must understand their sons how to have cleanliness and safe habits.

IMPOSE AN AMBITION FOR EDUCATION AND KNOWLEDGE

Your son needs to be trained if you like a mechanic, a hairdresser, or a neurosurgeon. Wisdom is power. The day we want to stop rising is the day we no longer have to know anything else, which is why, as a life-long endeavor, we will instill in our children that we are never terminated with knowledge and learning. Give your son always the joy and enjoyment of education and learning. Enable him to figure out the books will motivate him to do everything he likes.

Of starters, he may want Lacrosse's sport. He doesn't know much about the sport, so he looked at a game and decided to check it out and join a squad maybe. He should brace himself if he is able to learn about the sport.

The exercise of athletics is extremely important, but it is also useful to understand the rules and how to use the equipment correctly and what exercises make it a better player. Tracking a book at the Lacrosse Library will be of benefit to him before he goes on the field. In order to be good at it, he has to be able to master the sport.

Nevertheless, schools and books alone do not need to know. It's a product of life and mentorship. The urge to do something positive can only go as far as possible. We must always be able to learn and to develop by integrating accumulated expertise and experience.

TELL ABOUT LIMITS AND HOW TO RESPECT OTHERS

Boys are going to be men, never a valid reason for misconduct. Good behavior expectancy starts in the region. Children must be trained to honor others, especially elders and women, in particular. We will carry this conviction with them into their matriculations, jobs, and adult life because they are educated at home that women are inferior. When boys are told that women are equal to men, they tend to honor them.

Would that mean they have the same skills? Sorry, not that. Women can't give birth to children anymore. But that doesn't make us inferior with varying skills, and it just affects us.

Encourage men as boys to value women's strengths and values to support girls and children. In the future, it will also teach you to be a better friend, a better husband, an attraction for the same sex. If it is taught that women are less than men or that women do not need to be respected, it will probably be said and followed up by those thoughts. The driving force behind our actions is our emotions and convictions. Our actions transform into our life.

Within our culture, domestic abuse and sexual harassment are real and pervasive issues. Of much larger weight, the majority of criminals are men and women. Domestic Shelters is a domestic abuse awareness agency. They say 85 percent of victims of domestic abuse are women. People from childhood must be taught that abuse, in particular against women, is irrational. You must always be told that 'no' means 'no.' If a woman or a girl doesn't say anything about physical improvement, she should stop.

If children are taught to support young people, and it is taken to heart, it avoids abuse against women. But it should've been an ongoing dialogue during the youth and adolescent years to speak about how to handle women would not be a one-time discussion.

It is also important to provide good behavioral models and relationships. If a husband abuses his wife, sons who watch teach and learn this pattern of abuse. Tell your sons never hit a lady, but in the fitness of anger, you strike your mother. Your acts are going to talk louder than you think.

HAVE THEM DO ROUTINE PHYSICAL EXERCISE

It's not easy to raise girls. By the moment they're little children, they will be hard and tough with lots of potentials. I do that myself because I learn how to handle or regulate my twins for more regular strength. I realize they need lots of room and opportunities for physical fitness because most kids are physiologically so. Attempting to reduce resources because they expect substantial academic success is like hungering and anticipating a child to overeat.

In order to excel in school, children need more physical exercise. The game time in school is just not enough during the recess. The study has found that children require more physical activity than in leaves. It ensures that it is vital to run outdoors and play games, to get their aggression out before and after training. For long stretches, they were not forced to sit at the desks but would sit at school all day long. The answer is to make them work after school and before school if they have to sit down on a bench for a long time.

Kids lack physical exercise and are better likely to concentrate and pursue higher education every day and in reasonable periods of time. If they are not able to use their physical resources, they may have issues such as loss of attention, decreased academic success, difficulties reading, depression, anxiety, and frustration. Boys will be allowed out every day, several hours a day, and their physical strength.

GUIDE FOR RAISED BOYS FROM AGE TO ADULTHOOD

Most children exhibit different growth patterns, including in the womb. Their brains are growing weaker as they continue to develop testosterone in just a few months. So, the disparity continues – in certain facets of brain growth at five years of age, many guys are up to 20 months behind people. It's not only that but boys too different in size. Umbrian cord blood screening at the birth reveals that some babies are elevated and others low in testosterone. And high-testosterone boys find reading and communicating even more difficult. The general probability of children becoming trouble readers is three times higher than the trouble of students. And these are mainly high-testosterone babies.

Today, "girls are girls" is the last thing we would like to hear because they indeed are the worst of cop-outs. This means that we will say, "Yes, let us start reading this boy, telling him stories, reading books on bed and talking with him while we are on our day and listening to him." Don't dive him before a Television or a phone. The planet does not need people to fight buffalo again, but every child and every man must be in a position to talk. We will help our children grow up and get along with the boys.

The moment you looked into the eyes of your infant son, you realized that all your potential hope lies in your actions. Can you help him become a responsible, loving, positive man?

Every mother wonders how she does in the raising of her child. Yet you would still be the kind of guy you want your son to be if you follow the advice given below.

THE CHILDHOOD OF THE BABY

STOP STEREOTYPING SEXUALITY

'Young kids expect the world to be as straightforward as possible, making it easier for them to perceive the world by placing people in a pink or blue box,' but it is impossible to undo the mindset after it is created.

Instead, stop first teaching gender roles. Provide a range of toys and games, even if healthy for children. Provide books and films featuring female stereotypes as well as gender roles such as male nurses and women's athletes.

Be always mindful that you share the duties with your mates. You are taking turns to see what you do and how you deal with different relationships with your employer doing so-called female and male household work. The long-term payback for fighting gender discrimination. "Studies indicate that people with fewer sexual expectations record happy marriages and intimate relationships more optimistic."

TELL YOUR BOY ABOUT BOUNDARIES

Throughout this point, you don't need to go physically, but it is essential to let your son know at the earliest possible moment that he can decide, when and how, who should access his body?

This ensures that before kissing or touching anyone, including grandmother, must be granted permission. Don't push it if it refuses. (Sometimes it is nice to give a hug, handshake or high-five, or wave choice, but, again, to all three its's appropriate to say no.) And teach other people the same rights to him — without consent, he is not permitted to contact anyone or their property.

SCHOOL GOING BOYS
IMPEDE THE FEELING OF DOMINANCE

For one study, about 40 percent of boys for fourth grade became more intellectual than girls. They are promoting mixed-gender partnerships to avoid this line of thought. "The more you allow children to spend time in touch with girls and see them as individuals, the more likely it becomes for them to stereotype the entire group, or think boys are more successful," So this should not rely solely on gender. Teach him to view people concerning race, age, ethnicity, cultural-economic status, or sexual preference.

ENCOURAGE THEIR EMOTIONS

Never say "big boys don't complain" or "you behave like a child," but that kind of talking can potentially be harmful in addition to reinforcing gender roles. "The energy from an angry does not decrease or go away if boys cut off from genuinely expressing hurt feelings. It can lead to misbehavior and twitch how a boy thinks about himself and life in general," is non-profit that advocates social equity, men with traditional social, like mental concealment, are more likely to be distressed, suicidal thinking and depression. It is, therefore, essential to listen to your son and let him communicate his emotions.

If parents are trying to develop a relationship with their son under which he can reach them as collaborators. They can in, themselves from pressures that otherwise they will be forced to isolate him from their true selves, so they can help avoid the influence of peer culture — in the case of youth, of brotherhood.

MIDDLE SCHOOL BOYS
RAISE THEM TO MAKE HEALTHY INTERACTIONS
Data reveals that at least once a year after high school, nearly 90% of girls are sexually assaulted. The years at high school are a perfect time to warn your son that inappropriate remarks, jokes, or actions [to girls or boys] are never acceptable or unsuitable. Think about opportunities to communicate and keep your attention to find out what a good relationship feels.

Tell your kids to honor the option of the parent, regardless of the answer. "Ask him if the person's not involved, instead of asking why, he can respond, 'thank you for letting me know' - or attempt to modify the answer,"

The way to explain how your son deals with crushes is to illustrate how a solid friendship looks. Any of the things that you and your wife would like to highlight our shared love, commitment, and energy in the relationship, empathy, humility, and sympathy, and apologies for mistakes is very valuable. A research released in the Youth and Adolescence Review last year showed that young people living in a supportive family environment are more likely to overcome conflicts and less at risk for interpersonal conflict than young adults.

DOCILE ACTIONS OF "TOUGH MAN"

Social norms will sadly make adolescents feel strict, defensive, or even violent. "I know that a lot of the boys would think they have to be rough or strong, but there is another way to be a boy or a guy," your son says. "I don't know." You talk, instead, about sharing examples like older boys or people of your own family who respect or are sensitive and care for construction dispute resolution, or icons or other public officials, you trust pattern those habits."

Reduce your son's aggression and remind him that while rage and resentment are normal emotions, he cannot show them in ways that harm or physically threaten people. Support him to find reasonable ways to handle these feelings.

Gender-based discrimination is another problem that is associated with the so-called rough position of men. Women that are not super dominant don't show themselves verbally or assertively, or women that don't comment about boys get mocked because other girls label them derogatory slurs. Speak to your son and support him in finding ways to handle if he's at the edge. Call it out if your son allows the taunting. Remind him that there are many ways to be a human, and mocking or harassing a child isn't all right.

BOYS OF HIGH SCHOOL
BE EXPRESS ABOUT ACCEPTANCE
You no longer have to discuss questions of consent for high-school youth. They are determining what is called sexual assault, how to ask for approval, and how drugs and alcohol can affect a person's decision and consent. When older boys go to school with younger children, make sure that you have the correct age of consent in your country and period of partnership discrepancies.

STAY CONNECTED
The same recommendation applies because these children are teenagers, even because parents are encouraged to spend extra one-on-one time with their young children. "Go and lie down beside your son and play whatever he does, whether it's a match or a computer game." Boys also continue to use the time deliberately. "You can unload pressures, challenges, and deceptions and share

details about your inner world," says Martin. Maintaining a one-on-one relationship allows you to continue to assist him in handling the challenging issues as he reaches manhood.

COLLEGE GOING BOYS
GIVE HELPING HAND TO THEM

A solid, quiet man and the bad guy on the big screen the appeal, but the good guys are those in real life who have the right way of coping with their emotions. "Some characteristics we stereotypically assume are repressive — stocked and in charge, not expressing how you feel."

The study indicates that parents are telling their daughters to feel like they are more often than children, and when girls get hurt, they get support from their parents rather than from their boys. "They are tired, and you are not and bad. The outcome? Most kids turn into mentally insecure guys who can't relate well — fill in or out — which makes it impossible for them to bond with other people.

OPEN-TALKING

Don't come in with questions if your son is grumpy after classes. "Tell them plainly, 'Looks like you're angry. I'm just here to help,'" Then bring it up later: there is something terrible at school I'm concerned. If he sends you a little (School is annoying), he will express his feelings. The odds are that he'll wake up, that's how much homework my teacher gives me. Again, affirm your emotions, but persuade more this time: you have a lot to do at home. For tonight, what have you? "Your son will know you're by his side so that you won't be reading, and he can be confident communicating more," he explained.

PROVIDE HELP IN ANY SITUATION

It's one thing to have boys open up to feel, to make them realize that while bad feelings can hang on, they don't last. "Children, rather than feeling, tend to focus on the issue." "To tell your child the feelings — pain, sorrow, rage, anxiety — will not always go away easily is one of the parents' responsibility, and that is all right. He'll finally start to sound better."

TEACH YOUR CHILD RESPONSIVENESS

If kids understand how people feel, so they make better friends and happier husbands and dads in the future. "Empathy is a powerful cognitive ability that makes you feel good for people and prevents you from doing bad things," he said. "It's one of your son's strongest pillars." Research suggests, though, that moms will cut off their jobs. Students at the college today are 40 percent less empathic than 20 years earlier, according to analysts. The researchers suggest two possible factors are violent video games that bog children through the suffering of others, and social networks overflowing with children with imaginary "people."

PLAY WITH YOUR BOY

Motivate your boy to choose his shoes by providing examples of what he wants, such as athletics. When, for instance, he's watching a baseball match, join him on his sofa and say, "The starter seems to be under tremendous pressure." Where are you supposed to be on the mound? "It only takes a few seconds, so you encourage your son to look at the emotions of others and put himself in their stead," "If you do that consistently over the years, you will become someone who can cope emotionally well."

TELL HIM TO STUDY NOVELS

People are reading fiction scores higher for empathy assessments than non-fiction. How does this happen? Researchers are theorizing about the portions of the intellect that we use to understand the fictional personalities that we use to understand the genuine emotions of people. And the higher our capacity to comprehend the others using certain portions of our brain.

ENHANCE HIS SELF-SENSE

You are talking of personalities that you respect. The odds are essential: a good dose of self-esteem is a common trait. This doesn't mean a guy is greedy because he feels suitable for himself. He feels trustworthy, professional, and dignified, just what you want for your family.

DON'T PROMOTE WRONG ACTIVITIES

Saying that your son can't live up to you are the best kid in the world or that you are the greatest basketball player ever. "Look instead at his strengths," he says. Young children feel happier and satisfied because they are rewarded for the things they perform (You have worked hard) and complete it (Good job), and they are more able to tackle obstacles than when I am proud of you when you get the general kudos.

DO NOT MARK HIM

Don't say the boys will never be boys or use specific terms to condemn the behavior of your son or suggest his acts are not monitored. "The signals that children receive from parents play a critical role in improving their self-esteem," he says. "This hurts his credibility because your son knows the words he hits." Necessarily, he'll continue to accept what those sentences say — that kids are troublemakers.

TEACH TO RESPECT OTHERS

"A young boy who grows up listening to sources of authority, upholding laws and engaging knows the fundamentals of respecting others," When he is a child, he will be second nature in this respectful manner.

SET RULES AND REGULATIONS

If your son uses inappropriate words or loses a key or a similar breach, if your son violates a statute, enforce consequences. "The children admire people who keep their foot to the flames," she said. "When you coddle your son without seeing any repercussions, he will become over time demotivated, lazy and unscrupulous."

SET A GOOD EXAMPLE FOR YOUR BOY

In the life of your family, handle with respect other people such as teachers, coaches, and parents of his peers. Insist he's doing the same thing. If there is a disagreement, perhaps between your son and the teacher, approach the situation gracefully. Don't go with your son instantly. "Hear the story from all sides, and even though your child is right, tell him that a teacher's grossness is never appropriate," he says. Then say: I'm going to talk to your instructor to see if this can be fixed. I want your instructor to tell me if anything like this happens again. "You should show your son the ability to fix problems while respecting others,"

SHOW YOUR LOVE AND AFFECTION

Once he was young, his son enjoyed your hugs and kisses. It is common for children of this age to start withdrawing from their parents. Yet note, people who give love have grown up to find means of expressing it to your son — even if he does not want you to be like him.

SET A TIME TABLE
Use your time wisely while your son refuses. When you want to kiss him in front of his friends, he might be humiliated, but the quick choice when he goes to bed, or a brief hug when he feels sad, would let him know that you care without crowding. "The kids like and want the mother's loving presence, even though they don't always demonstrate it," she said. "Being affectionate men, boys will feel this physical responsiveness."

FATHER'S RESPONSIBILITY
Dad has a distinct edge over Mom when it comes to parenting boys: he knows where the kid comes from because of his race. "Surely a mother can support a son, but a father will teach him what it means, and that's important," he said.

Sounds too simple, but for a son, it's essential to have a parent who spends time with him, "Warren said. Boys get a message that dad loves me, likes my company, and is there any time I need him, that's what gives them a sense of confidence and shows what good fathers do.

I handle people. Nice treat women. One way a boy knows how to communicate with women is by looking at his brother. "If the dad engages with women and his wife, in particular, he should be willing, especially during an argument, to admit that he is wrong, apologize, talk, and behave respectfully."

Get fit. Get comfortable. Studies show that many fathers share with their children the kind of aggressive wresting and hard living that allows boys to restrain their physical urges and to manage their emotions. "Furthermore, a dad who embraces and kisses his son profoundly declares his intimate presence."

CHAPTER 9: BREAK FREE OF THE OVERPARENTING TRAP & PREPARE KIDS FOR SUCCESS

Currently, many parents refuse to give their children free reception while they are kids to play alone outdoors or on the playground. They create adults who struggle to protect themselves. In the process, they create.

On the other side, some parents go to the lengths that they have their children's schoolwork just to make sure their little kids excel. Julie suggests that students are practically treated as a regular activity to do jobs that their parents do while their teachers appear otherwise.

"Yes, of course, closeness, affection, love, frequent communication between parent and offspring, that's all good. Who among us wouldn't wish for a closer relationship with our parents?"

You have to avoid cutting their meat anywhere if you want your child to be independent at 18 years. But when are you done meat cutting? When do you avoid searching for both ways when crossing the street? When are you encouraging them to talk to strangers?

This omnipresent over-implication means that the children become adults in chronology while remaining stunted, dependent on their parents not only to lift their lives slowly, but also on lovely, light, and ethereal dreams.

The best thing is—not just the pride of charting the course in others. The morality slip-ups in overhauling their schoolwork, the brutality of being a relentless crutch, the damage that comes from turning love into performance—the worst parts are this secret message that we give to children: – 'I don't think you should. The best part is this cryptic message, which we offer to children, we over help them so that they are not weak, but since we do too much, they are degraded.

In this life, you're not strong enough; that's the message.

You're never going to be.

You're still going to need me.

Some creators – count me here – are aware that we are still taking incentives for children to build the types of skills and values that developed in the earliest days of their lives. As they run smartphones and participate in social media, they have encountered intense academics long before formal schooling. The real issue is that forcing our children too hard to "advance" and "complete." We decrease the fundamentals of learning, which encourages children to become doers — people who can handle what will be an unpredictable future and who are preparing to identify, achieve, and secure their dream of success. They don't have to remove all conventional aspects of growing up now, but we should guarantee that the foundational moments children do not get rid of this.

CHILDREN WILL DISCOVER THE PLANET
Children will spend a lot of time engaging, chatting, and playing with adults by their hands. Kids need to expose themselves to stimuli to interact with the environment, sometimes like a Children's Museum, where discovery without limits, however, welcomed, is not just perfect. So much programmed play – and time spent with the app – reduce the simple learning in unstructured sports. So the focus on "academics" early in childhood goes against decades of study into how the brain evolves (whether it is a recession, pretends, playing school) at the cost of playing.

LEARNING WITH INNOVATIONS
Children are solvers of fundamental problems. We test theories about cause and effect and understand what is more about trial and error. These skills can be promoted or quashed by adults. Children require freedom to perform free, unstructured events. Drawing pictures, using

construction blocks, molding clay, and every other ability for a child to work without guidance and feedback help the children explore their creative selves. Parents will facilitate this cycle by having opportunities with clear resources to unstructured opportunities and by promoting and supporting the excitement of learning and the pleasure of drawing beyond the lines.

CHILDREN TODAY BENEFIT FROM OPTIMISM

People learn how to deal and function with approaches, which are maybe not panaceas, but resilience. Parents may empower children to think about their problems – whether it is learning to drive a bike without training wheels, the challenging school class, a friend's dilemma – and help them discuss what can be done and determine the next steps for progress.

CHILDREN ARE OPPORTUNITY HUNTER

Children do not learn to behave in the cover of the bubble — but neither should they be irresponsible. Instead of relying on "risk-taking," teaching children to pursue opportunities to learn how to do so while handling the possible downsides (to learning from them), people should understand the advantages of challenging themselves. It may be "hand-off, but eyes on," if a child tries to climb a tree a little high. Not just athletic exercise, it's not. Make sure that a kid has a confident hand-raising in class even though she doesn't know the solution.

Teach a child, it's all right to try playing at school, also though they are a little shy while they are on stage. Celebrate commitment and prosperity instead of "major gains."

CHILDREN SHOULD TAKE FILTHY JOBS

How do children perform tasks? Children should not only be able to pitch in age-appropriate ways but recognize that you cannot trust someone else to do all the dirty jobs. Let children play their part in family activities and learn about working with others to do what they need, without having to do things they are not equipped to do alone. Make them know that the world is not about you, and those who continue to do their grunting jobs are becoming productive men.

SOCIAL SKILLS ARE MANDATORY

We continue to work on forecasting success as an adult (personal and professional) by learning how to get along with other children early in life. Children must know how to handle disputes instead of stumping and shouting proactively. Working together is a skill that is nurtured through childhood, and it will inspire parents to take turns to work together as a team that encourages them to supports a mission. Communication is important-it pays off later on in other respects to speak to children and to improve their communication skills at all ages.

KIDS SHOULD HELP OTHERS

Evidence shows that children – including girls – become potential helpers when they are given a chance. When you spill it, see if your child can pick it up and leave it. They just need a thank you in return. Some research shows that supporting a child as a "healthy friend" fosters a feeling of caring for others. Explicate how we will all consider means of helping those in need, and model empathy and consideration. The ideas for raising a Can-do Child were recommended to contribute to "lasting outcomes." The laptops and piano lessons would not be omitted. Make sure that you give your kid ample time to develop all of the skills at home they will use to support them as they leave their nests.

WAYS TO AVOID OVERPARENTING

One of the most robust but most lucrative occupations on the planet is to be a father. Responsibility for another's survival may appear terrifying or intimidating, and it may exhaust you. Overpaid children frequently make their own choices or live alone in hardship. By helping your child, growing confidence and resilience, fixing challenges, you can prevent that.

Excessive parenthood. That's what we all want. Why will the loop be interrupted? Learn about four measures to avoid being over-friendly and offer your children the best opportunities to be positive, healthy, and prosperous.

In the first two-part show, we find out that flying, helicoptering, and micromanagement are another term ignoring. It is termed over parenting when parents do what they should and can do for their babies. It's over-parenting when you try to correct or discourage errors of your children.

We have looked at two (more or less) explanations that most of us do this: the quest for college and the fear of dangerous and self-harming behaviors.

HOW IS YOUR CHILD AFFECTED BY THE OVERPARENTING?

The fundamental concern is that children will commit errors and mistakes that are irreparable. It's called tragic, imaginative, and future-oriented rather than peacefully solving the problem. The kids use the phrase, "I don't think you can handle anything yourself, so I'm going to have to do something for you" as adults do not overprotect. Finally, the kids continue to accept that, yet another reasonable justification for avoiding over parenting.

This message and conviction paralyze our children from partnerships to schools, from activities to work. You slowly stop talking about yourself and stop solving problems. Why worry when Dad knows and shows you the right way to do it? You know that you don't have to be sorry for yourself. And if Mama can't bear it to do it for you? Why pick your filthy clothes up from the ground? What happens when your parents try to lessen the results or transfer the blame to own an issue at school?

Another consequence is that they are avoiding harm. We take no positive risks: a course in AP which may be tested to receive a B rather than an A, and seeks to act that they do not excellently, including filling the dishwasher, as it is not achieved to the satisfaction of a parent. You refuse any options because they may be the "fake" ones.

If you have ever found that, particularly with your kids, when things aren't perfect, your body's reaction is to do more, not less? You will raise your voice instead of dropping it if you don't care. If they struggle with the hard, instead of being quiet or giving only a few suggestions, you leap in with tons of ideas. In reality, though, a smoother voice would attract their focus more efficiently, and proposing less of your suggestions would inspire you to formulate all your strategies.

There is an apparent belief in our society that when our children struggle, they need more focus, more energy, more effort, and more compassion. Lately, Johnny looks a bit day-dreamy, perhaps his parents need more attention. Each semester, Jessie doesn't do well enough in classes, so she wants teachers and parents to concentrate on something. Or Emma seems to have no self-esteem, so maybe she wants more attention, appreciation, and acceptance.

AVOID DEFEAT, SPECULATION AND EXCESS SHARING

Perhaps that applies to specific children and individual guardians, but it's not valid much of the time. It is also an excellent way to hinder our children from providing one of these things. And if we act out of love in this manner, we will create the exact opposite result. Instead of self-reliance, we unconsciously encouraged dependency. Kids become hooked. So we parents often get our satisfaction by feeling supportive so crucial for our children by over-doing. Yet they eventually know impotence instead of toughness.

OUR CHILDREN'S TOLERANCE

We also learn that it is essential to meet the desires and feelings of others to be a successful parent, spouse, or mate. Yeah, that's significant, but only to a certain degree.

When the reaction is more:

Was it better than fewer now, then? Some of the examples are there.

1) Do more about yourself and your kid less. In this situation, it is a more compassionate and conscientious approach to take for a mom to do less empathizing and "meeting their needs" and less emphasis on her.

2) Less concern about satisfying the needs of the children and more encouraging them to take responsibility for themselves. Think less of the

children's emotions and more about making them act in the best possible way. For example, "I'm no longer going to learn, and you can get the missed homework books — you have to figure out what is right tomorrow or do it." "You do not want to confess to your cousin that you're sorry, but I hold you responsible for doing the right thing."

3) Talk less about buying and grumbling and more about controlling and governing themselves. "I know you dislike your jobs, so I want them to be done before I ask you to do them. You may be sad, but please don't find a way to drag anyone down if you're unsatisfied.

Always be with your children in the way they need you, but otherwise, step away from them. And learn to appreciate the gap.

When professors, attorneys, and relatives tell you that your children appear to need more from you — attention, patience, energy, compassion, compassion — stop thinking hard. Should they do? Will you ignore them? If so, you can, of course, do better than you can. Yet they get more than enough from you in the possible case. It is also safer for if you cut to make legs impossible to find. Letting go will first make you feel wobbly, but you're going to find your heavy legs standing with practice and time.

1) You should admit that you have learned the most of your life from 'failures' and deceptions. Recall why these aren't deadly. Offer your child the gifts of deceit and mistake.

2) Take a deep breath and ask yourself, "Whose is the problem? Either your child is wrong, or you want to step in to avoid one? "If this is (and sometimes is) your child's question, step back. Let him handle it if it is not a matter of health or welfare. He will know how he can repair himself or take responsibility for the consequences. He will discover who he is. When he wants to be there, you should be on the sidelines.

3) Grant your kids an acceptable age for home management duties. You must know that life is more than just grades and the road to college. It needs all family members to run their house and home smoothly, and they must gain useful abilities to live alone.

4) Most options aren't 'forever.' The possibilities of today can be traded tomorrow for another chance. Let the children know that they still have opportunities while waiting for them to take steps and achieve their goals.

SIGNS THAT YOU ARE THE CHILD'S OVERPARENT

Overparenting corresponds to the efforts of a parent to micro-manage the life of their infant. Stubbornly circling the infant to make wise choices, to shield them from any physical or mental distress, and to discourage them from owning up to the effects of their actions, are some of the over-protective parent's moral priorities.

The inability of a parent to control their distress is typically the product of over-parenting because they cannot accept watching their child hurt, lose, or making mistakes. Parents frequently feel ashamed of punishment and fail to enforce the effects of punishment on their children. Continued hyper-vigilance and overindulgence may have significant effects, for example, stunting the growth of an infant and making an infant excessively dependent.

BELOW ARE THE MOTTLED SYMPTOMS OF THE CHILD'S OVER-PARENTHOOD:

YOU'RE GOING THROUGH SMALL POWER STRUGGLES

Historical power struggles may mean that you are too picky or too challenging. You could discourage her from gaining the independence she would need if you argue with a 5-year-old about eating enough food, or if you clash with your 15-year-old over how she styles her hair.

YOU START TO MAKE YOUR CHILD'S PREFERENCES

Often, there's the "only approach" or the "correct way" to do it, so that will contribute to your child's micro-management. You are over-parenting because you can't let your kid try new possibilities, for instance, to wear clothes not appropriate for him or to place a bath in the roof while playing in his dollhouse.

YOU CAN NOT BEAR TO SEE THE LOSS OF YOUR CHILD

No one wants to see their child lose, so they won't benefit from their failures if you run in and save the children if they have difficulties. Whenever they have trouble finding their homework or interfere with the first hint of a question on a play date, your child does not improve question-solving skills if you can give them the correct solution.

Kids often have to feel defeat on their own. Recovering from disappointment allows kids to figure out if they can do it better in the future.

YOU'RE CONCERNED ABOUT OTHER PARENTS' ISSUES

If you are the only person who is always worried about your six years old, who is playing on the playground's monkey bars? But you do not bear the thought of a 13-year-old who crosses the street with friends, so it may be enticing to believe that it is because you're more compassionate than the other adults. Yet consider the risk of over-parenting before drawing the inference. You could manipulate them to their full capacity if you don't treat your child like an intelligent, capable person.

YOU DISAGREE OVER HOW YOUR CHILD IS HANDLED WITH ADULTS

You could be over-parenting because you regularly debate their rules with parents, coaches, daycare providers, and other guardians about how the infant is treated. Irresponsible parents also phone teachers to suggest a better grade for their child or forbid Grandma from encouraging children to eat sugar.

Trying to micro-management is not as safe as other people often abuse your kids. In different settings, children benefit from learning various rules.

YOU ARE UNABLE TO RECOGNIZE ACCEPTABLE AGES

Overpricing is always the product of excessively high aspirations. For starters, a parent may engage a child in hundreds of activities and may also handle free time for a child to make sure she is still thriving.

Sometimes, unacceptable outcomes arise because parents have too low aspirations. Mothers who do not believe their child should act individually will do anything – including their homework – because they don't know for their kids.

YOU DON'T OFFER MANY DUTIES TO YOUR CHILD

Unnecessary treatment is also like an excessive indulgence. You won't develop life skills if you don't delegate jobs, or if you don't want them to be autonomous. It will only be a long time if your kid is spared from liability.

It's not safe to discipline your child so that you don't have any fear. The independence for your child to be a kid is vital. Overparenting will discourage your child from going through a rich and full childhood to train for a more mature adult.

YOUR BABY DRESSING

Put your hand up if the kid's clothes already get gathered up, encourage them to put on, and assist them with zips, buttons, socks, and shoes. Culpable?

Your child will be able to dress up by three years of age, and though he needs assistance by buttons before he smoothers his motor skills. Allow your child to select his or her outfit instead of choosing what your child is going to wear. When he gets older, give him a little more flexibility before he's fully confident.

My child's fashion choices we don't always agree with, but we want to note that his clothes are a means of self-expression. Although his clothes are clean and respectable (even though he doesn't like it), let him wear whatever he wants.

CONCLUSION

I hope that the people would emulate the great learning displayed by this presentation.

Exploring children's books: words and images, this free course has demonstrated the illustrations in children's books are not mere immature items but are always considered to be unchallengeable. Readers may use nuanced cultural awareness to make sense of them. Many childhood illustration critics point out that the pictures themselves are complex and imaginative, as well as the number of diverse ways in which they blend visuals with words for stories. In certain instances, photographs and materials in children's books are not merely by-products; they are essential to the story growth.

COPYRIGHTS

The information provided here is correct and reliable, as any lack of attention or other means resulting from the misuse or use of the procedures, procedures, or instructions contained therein is the total, and absolute obligation of the user addressed.

The author is not obliged, directly or indirectly, to assume civil or civil liability for any restoration, damage, or loss resulting from the data collected here. The respective authors retain all copyrights not kept by the publisher.

The information contained herein is solely and universally available for information purposes. The data is presented without a warranty or promise of any kind.

The trademarks used are without approval, and the patent is issued without the trademark owner's permission or protection.

The logos and labels in this book are the property of the owners themselves and are not associated with this text.

HOW TO RAISE AN ADULT

Prepare your kid For Success! How to Raise a Boy, Break Free of the Overparenting Trap, increase your Influence with The Power of Connection to Build Good Men

By

James Goodchild

TABLE OF CONTENT

the written permission of the publisher and all liberties authorized.

The information provided here is correct and reliable, as any lack of attention or other means resulting from the misuse or use of the procedures or instructions contained therein is the total and absolute obligation of the user addressed.

The author is not obliged, directly or indirectly, to assume civil liability for any restoration, damage, or loss resulting from the data collected here. The respective authors retain all copyrights not kept by the publisher.

The information contained herein is solely and universally available for information purposes. The data is presented without a warranty or promise of any kind.

The trademarks used are without approval, and the patent is issued without the trademark owner's permission or protection.

The logos and labels in this book are the property of the owners themselves and are not associated with this text.

INTRODUCTION

When did children prepare themselves for success with the core purpose of parenting? The inherent uncertainty of a global capitalist society and its unbending focus on wealth and the future represent this dominant ideology. It demands that any act of parenting to be judged on the grounds of whether a child can contribute to a life of achievement or failure. No wonder parenting encourages a heated discourse because of the ambiguous application of these concepts in youth. What remains if an increasing dietary operation is performed in the far future? A child who is saturated in the ambient anxiety which accompanies any simple choice or action is an anxious child created in his concerned parent's hand-ringed, future-oriented image. They do not teach babies, and they raise adults.

It is a subtle but significant distinction. Kids can be obedient or fearful, but that does not mean they will do what is best when they venture out on their own. To raise kids who become great adults, you must instill such character traits in them that will inform their future decisions and actions. One of the easiest ways of ensuring that your kids are prepared to cope with maturity is to show them how to deal with their money now. Wealth is not just wealth; instead, it tends to be a way of life.

You teach child accountability when you put a child to work

That's how it requires follow-up, the best intentions, and transparency that can be the jobs in the house or employment at the mall. Work demonstrates that your daughter manages her decisions herself and will enjoy the perks of her career. Successful adults are in control.

You advise them to use wisdom while telling a child to invest

It is fun to spend money. Children understand this. Your son learns that, yes, it is fun to spend money, but he has also known that it should be done with caution. Intelligent investment requires sound judgment and a critical quality in life too. Reasonable grownups are using intelligence.

You show them courage as they ask a child to save

In a world of escapism, children are growing up. Saving capital slows children down. Perhaps a little wounded, but that's all right. Saving money will teach your daughter that when she wants it, she cannot get what she needs high endurance with adults.

You teach them kindness if you ask a child to share

Generosity is described as being able to share. However, many children do not find it necessary. As a mom, inspire your child to behave and watch the heart evolve. Generosity is an essential weapon to counter egoism and greediness.

You show them sincerity as you tell a kid to stop liability

Debt enables people to exploit. You will purchase a larger house with loans, drive a more exceptional car, and host lavish dinners. Just as your daughter wants to escape debt for good, she would need to be truthful about what she will do and who she truly is, with herself and with everyone around her. Proper grown-ups are truthful.

If you teach a kid to be satisfied, you show thankfulness to him

Material emerges from an understanding that God holds everything. He builds everything we have and all we are. Children will be all right about how God made them and being He is giving them to do as they understand this idea. It is just a perk for anything else. If your son is happy, he will always be grateful. Competent adults demonstrate thankfulness. The argument is that for kids and teenagers, there is a countdown to maturity, and the time will not end. What sort of adults do you create, is the real question? This problem will inspire us to continue to respond to our children with a reason. When I thought about my youth, I remember how they were my role models. They inspired me to make an effort to be a kind hostess.

It was not easy when I tried to mix maternity and work. The children are also conscience-extensions. That is true, regardless of whether they are native or transported. Often claimed, "blood thicker than water," but not always enough to make Step-Dad's intense affection towards her foster daughter clear. When it comes to parenting, you want the best for your babies. That is why the whole family life will not be forgotten, and it is a quick hop to the next level. But what would you say to your children when you have your service in order? The dream of any parent is a healthy and stable child. Creating an infant is an act of consciousness that nobody succeeds unintentionally.

You seem to want your relationship to continue when trying to achieve your ambitions, but why would you do that without debilitating your kids?

It is true because you did not want to do it yourself. Why are you building templates in your children, without becoming a tyrant, to develop trust and to succeed? The following results are taken into account. Raising a child is not easy. As adults, we always dream about what our kids want, but we never ask what they want. However, as we consider what they mean, we find that we just have to do what often children say. We assume that we know better about what we do and therefore draw the right decisions. Each parent needs to grow up safe and happy children. Yet there is not much parenting guidance out there. Who are you going to hear, and what advice is reliable? All these questions arise in the mind of every parent. Children are the significant assets of parents.

Consequently, they want their children to show their best in every situation. But this is possible with the help and the guidance of parents. Children are the mirror image of their parents.

If you want your kids to be responsible for people, please give them the jobs. I am sure that it might sound like an overly basic platitude, but many of us continue to over-parent and over-lead. Have you ever learned that individual trees cast so much a shadow around them that nothing else can grow? Here are several ways to guarantee that your children will develop into mature adults:

Secure them from physical or mental discomfort of all sorts.

- Offer your apology for not running.
- Try to ensure them do anything you can do for them.

- Only give them what is going to make them happy.

In reality, the only way to ensure children grow up to be successful adults is to give them something that makes them happy as adults. Yet you should carry on obligations as you want them done as adults. The vital term is accountability.

It denotes two terms: Ability, reaction, and responsiveness. Can you see the relation between these two concepts? If you want to train children to become responsible, then guide them towards the right way of working and doing stuff. At any point, give them chores. This action demonstrates their willingness to respond.

Before they do it, the children never believe in what they can do. Empower them by giving them regular opportunities to understand what they should do. You could ruin a chance if you take it off too early or step in for them so that they feel necessary about what they have done. Do not be naive. Do not be impractical. You will certainly not be asking a young boy for a fence to create in the backyard. Or challenge a teenager to push a second. Using common sense and understand its strength. We do not recommend putting too much pressure or liability on anyone.

One of the essential values connected with obligation was something that Jesus said in a parable, "When you are loyal with a little, you will be trustworthy with a lot."

So how are you going to provide your children with interactions that train them for mature adults?

Now Keep at It

It can be sleepy, and you sometimes note the words are delivered in one accent. Contrarily, the studies have found that children are more likely to come to their parents with high expectations. That has been a triumph, and several big pitfalls have avoided.

A study of 15,000 people, aged 13 and 14 and 23-24 years old, showed that those with consistently high children's ambitions were:

1) More probably to become a graduate student.

2) Unable to get pregnant as teens.

3) Sin extended stretches of work probable.

4) Without all the incentive to be stuck in imperious, low pay jobs.

The argument was that the adolescents did not need to hear all the "high standards" and would not often react to it openly and honestly. But they discovered it at the end of each day. According to a survey, "Adolescent girls will do better if they have pushy mothers."

Praising Is Mandatory

In two crucial respects, parents esteem their children. The first is due to the innate skills. The second is due to their deeds. For example:

 1) Lobbies on skills: great job! For example, you're so good-looking! You're too bright!

2) Lobbying incentive: Fantastic service! You existed and learned!

3) Significantly higher front: praise kids, not abilities for their acts. You encourage and support them. Retake a look if you are a relatively young dad, and conclude that it is more appropriate because your kids are younger. The impacts of these reward techniques are evaluated only by infants between the age of 1 and 3.

Allow Kids to Go for Fun

When the weather is clear, it is fun for the kids and you. Remember this: we all who tend to work in the office have said that we are killed every day. So, what should we do for our children to do for six or seven hours? Take your place in the teachings. Science shows you can empower them to play outside as quickly and efficiently as possible. More the kids spend their time pretending, less effort they spend on aerobic exercise, and thus they increase their literacy over the years.

Allow Them to Do Jobs

I guarantee that it is a real piece. Why are we establishing job ethics in young children? It is what you have got: you make food, you're grassing, taking the rubbish out, going to the house, cleaning the rooms-everything kids steal at times, parents need to touch base for them. You had always seen how the dishwasher looked when you asked a 9-year-old to fill it. Have you ever had to brush the dog with a bunch of plastic bags after your seven years old walked? Yeah, well. Everything is right. Everything is good. The point is that if you did yourself, particularly in the early stages, it would be much simpler.

Behavior Success

You will be the first time your child has been in touch worldwide and have a significant effect on him (May I use the word of men to describe each gender). You are the first contact a child has in the world and at home as a dad. As Olukayode Alfred rightly said, "The first connection is that you have a child in your life." A happy parent makes a happy child; healthy kids do the same. You are a healthy and delicious person, the very first phase to growing a peaceful and happy child.

Set a Timetable for Family

You will take care to teach a decent child to the family as well. Your family needs time to speak out. The family bond is reinforced. Give your family a moment, even children, to feel at home. You can overcome problems, lift the mountains when you are satisfied with people. This is the cornerstone of developing a safe and happy child.

Manage some time for your family and children. This is a healthy activity to raise a successful adult.

Arrange Family Meals
There is a balanced environment around the table. It is an excellent shimmer. Make sure you have time to sit with your family and relatives. Ensure you make family meals every day. It does not happen daily. Just three breakfasts and four lunches should be eaten over a week. Cooked food is excellent in the kitchen, and with your babies, you can spend more time. You should take breakfast together.

Little Achievements Must Be Celebrated
A twilight zone makes a happy child. Families who honor the accomplishments of their parents are much healthy and wealthier. Kids from these homes tend to be more competitive in comparison to houses where wins are not a priority. You will enjoy the promotion, good points, awards, and other excellent stuff.

Solve Problems Wisely
You must know that the state of your home affects your kids. Unaddressed conflicts with children from their families rarely perform academically well. All of them have issues with friends and kids. This thing usually contributes to crime, drinking, substance addiction, anxiety, and other social problems. Freeze if you have a concern in your house as long as possible. The

happiness and success of your child is a significant factor.

Pay Attention to Children
The four-year-old, on average, poses more than 200 questions during the day. Is it not ideal that the replies he or she gets were generated, orally, and not verbally? The two-way interactions are the sharing of information between the parties concerned. Offer him your special treatment when your kid talks with you. This means that you have friendly eyes and understand him genuinely. You would have to describe what to do at that moment.

Manage Emotions According to Situations
You must learn, I mean, by talking and teaching them. You could concentrate only if your child is healthy emotionally. He would not be carried down easily or trapped in rash actions. Corporal and mental health are improved. Make sure your child is mindful of every feeling, but not every effort is suitable. Understand and sympathize with your child, explain for yourself, and respect your child's success.

Set Sound Rules
Healthy children are born in a law-abiding household. The first part is: children want to be safe. Kids, who are treated with negligible attitude, often tend to feel that parents do not care. It is terrible for children. They are either

alone or close. This is dangerous. We seem as stressed as we get out of balance for the first time.

Set Time for Rest

Any of the effects of sleep deprivation are hypertension, decreased brain activity, and diminished productivity. Take the time to relax and regain energy for your kids. Make sure your child has plenty of time to sleep well. Take the remainder of the night to make sure it suits them. Restrict screen hours and overnight activities that can interrupt your sleep. You should also catch an afternoon snack during your holiday. A relaxed mind is typically better than that and adds to the success and joy of a child.

Play Activity Is Must for Kids

Parents make some mistakes by not encouraging their children to play. Jack is a dull kid who plays no games. To make his child happy and successful, you will support his child to play freely. Motivate him to play outdoor games too, not just video or indoor activities. Whenever you can perform Board games and other videogames, make sure it suits soccer and track. This thing guarantees his mental and physical growth.

Reduce Time to Watch TV

Studies have shown that time spent on TV and the internet has a different connection. There are some examples, though, as for broadcast staff. Adults and teens are more worried about this time on TV. Be a perfect example, and actively restrict TV viewing. Seek to rest or talk wlth your children throughout the day.

Create Reading Interest in Your Child

Somebody had got a weird way of thinking. Teach your child to read this yourself. You could add a bit of reward to your child by the book successfully. You will read other books, including fantasy, history, business, and the work of your child's textbook. Your kids can read it. Stories are like an analytical fuel that promotes critical thinking development and imagination. Make use of the right books and make your child a happy, successful adult.

Consider the Outcomes of Any Activity

Do not make the error and think about the performance. Make sure you explain to your child the value of the results. Therefore, you will inspire your child to always live up to the excellent standard. Thus, children are getting more gradually. Look out for your child's actions even though you do not achieve the perfect result.

Ask Your Child to Develop New Relations

No one is just going to stay alone. There has to be a relationship. You should know how to build your child's positive relationship. It will help him and drive him towards success. To establish friendships with your kids, you have to create an atmosphere where you can test friendships with anyone else.

Teach Your Child Not to Be Selfish
Manufacturers assume that their lives are self-worthy, and they respect others. One approach is to teach the children selflessness. Inspire a healthy person. Teach them to be a helping hand for others when they need you in a difficult situation.

Take to See Attentions
Promote self-serve commands and endorse them. Allow your child to volunteer if family, school community resources are open. Do not forget to take your child while volunteering with you. Motivate your child to help and serve others as an adult, as a team or as a family.

Do not Shout at your Child
There is practically no justification for a boy who knows his right from the wrong. Shouting often creates more issues than can be fixed, so why to yell first. Your semi-teen can lack confidence and become accustomed to yelling. Crying is an unhealthy environment symptom, and children from these homes are likely to distrust and feel afflicted. When your child learns emotional maturity, you will still do so. Stop or leave the

room until you are quiet if you are on the line of tears. Do not apologize to your known kid until you worry about situations and agree. You want to be a confident, safe, and happy kid. Along with this, you also want their disappointment to understand and tell them why you have decided to do so.

Give Importance to Forgiveness over Punishment

There is less chance of people who will not forgive. Unforgiving challenges are real and genuine with joy, aside from appeasing human beings. It is doubtful that anyone would get a second chance without salvation. Make sure you agree with the positive behavior by removing the bad ones. Compassion is typically accomplished and less likely to feel upset or discouraged.

Learn Kid to Think Positive

Appreciation, joy, and social activities go hand in hand. The reality is nobody would be happy for a positive perspective. Get a bright outlook and let your children see that in you. Do not even make a massive deal for a minute. Then, maintain a specific perspective and talk. Tell your child the bright side of the black cloud. You remain optimistic and therefore speak on the bright side of life. Young minds are crystal clear. You must polish their mind with productive and positive things.

Be Supportive Parents & Provide them Guides

He needs other hands to help him as long as you see your child. Help him find and assist him in seeking a mentor. Confident parents are growing their chances of success in the life of a teen. Your mentor can be a trustworthy colleague, teacher, or family member.

Mistakes Are Acceptable

Fortunately, your child will not make any mistakes in their life. Fortunately, the ethics your kid needs to add to the growth. What do you think is the safest way of raising your child? It will never be off and will never expect Biplanes. To grow up, to be educated, and to give this experience a value? Finally, if you took the first option, you will limit your liberty. Your child must be able to acknowledge mistakes. They have provided that they are always presented, and never considered as the vital point in their narrative. Overall, they will never lose, even though they fail, because they make a mistake. The safest thing you can say is to remove the defects.

Try & Try

Your boy does not need to be the best singer, swimmer, or athlete. They do not have to be the brightest in their part-time workplace. Oh, children do not have to learn to compose until they are ten years old. They do not have to be Mr. Olympia or an excellent start in the annual competitions, but you have to do everything with an order for accomplishments in a better way. If you make it clear, the unnecessary pressure will be lowered and encourage them to start going and progressing. You would not be weighted down. It should just be secure. For starters, if you opt for these top 15 new NAMM 2020 products, you would be encouraged to invest in your hobby and passion.

Permit Kids to Live Accordingly

You must create a name for yourself. We are optimistic about the future if you approve it, which would be ideal if you decide to accept the motion. It all depends on the perspective. Primarily, with these tips, you will have a happy kid. Ironically, this improves the chances of success with your profession. You have got an enormous influence on your kids. However, I am not going to do that, so you should not start shaping now or later. I have called "the kid effects" the first point, although you are not sure about it, that you are influenced directly. He understands how you communicate with others (including the child) by the acts of sleep-speaking. This is why some kids would behave like their parents.

Were you aware that the inability to educate adults rather than children is the reason many parents are struggling to watch their adult children live in difficulty? Or why is a parent's mental distress well justified if they cannot finish sleeping because the adult needs to sleep a 25-year-old adult returning to their homes?

Why am I putting the responsibility on the shoulders of the parent? Since the parent is the one who trains the child for the real world, the coach is the dad. Father is the most incredible mentor of his children. Boys always follow their fathers to take steps in life. They think like their fathers.

A Popular Problem

Understanding your children is the main task in life. It is easy to see and feel both the pain when parents talk about this issue. It is incomprehensible. Some parents cannot understand their children well. Misunderstanding creates conflicts. Conflicts generate bad behavior between parents and children.

The Main Problem

It is reckless to raise children and accept them as though they are eternal babies because parents are not trained in intelligent parenthood. This is a real problem. A significant percentage of parents nurture their children as if they are forever kids out of arrogance, carelessness, or incompetence. They do not get the sense of Andy Andrews as he said: This thing suggests that the entire parent does in the course of raising a child will be undertaken to instill values or create a framework for influencing future choices and actions of the child. When you have a person, who cannot face the obstacles or hardships of life, this means that this person lacks the foundation or the characteristics that are required for effectively coping with such difficulties.

Adult Upbringing Means Teaching Children about Money

The training of children to develop into better adults ensures that they are educated about life. Capital principles also encourage children to invest, which provides that they learn to use wisdom. On the other hand, saving lessons help children become compassionate adults. Curriculum lessons will not be complete without the importance of sharing as children who know to be charitable.

Child Parenting Requires Showing Children the Importance of Hard Work

All the people who have to face a career challenge or a job challenge, the most important theme is their laziness. This routine shows lazy thought, lazy behavior, or just lazy all around. If a life challenge has an antidote, be it political, medical, or spiritual, it is hard work. Intelligent parents understand this and actively seek to instill proper respect in their children for working hard. Active and determined parents always try to take chances for their children.

Criticism Involves Showing Children How Well They Can Do Everywhere They Are

People from all walks of life are doing any job or work as if God himself had ordered them to accomplish their mission. They do their best, irrespective of whether their work is to scrub a toilet or write a company plan worth millions of dollars. The attitude to a mission that is still limited or significant is a function that is placed in childhood at the same degree of excellence. Due to this, the responsible parents should never handle this when their children do half an ass to wash their clothes or to cover the floor or some other homework. You know it continues into maturity to take only little life or death roles.

Child Education Is Conscientious Teaching

One research has found that the most significant trait that parents want their children to embody is "to be responsible." The explanation that children should be taught to be responsible is that accountability impacts every part of life. It influences physical wellbeing, mental health, economy, marriages, jobs, and all other aspects of life. The positive news about teaching children to be responsible citizens is that many incentives are available at home. Responsible parents realize that their children are often given repetitive activities, which are perfect ways to teach them. These parents are also taking these activities seriously because the experiences they learn in adulthood are practical.

Parent Raising Means Children Are Encouraged to Be Autonomous

The capability of standing on two feet is a characteristic that is absent in other adults. As a result, they rely on banks to lend them money, families for financial assistance, and credit card firms to buy necessities that they can pay. Intelligent parents teach their children freedom.

Tips for turning an independent teen into a mature adult

Most parents dream of a caring, confident youth, who gives a hand without being told to work with household chores, often calls to inspect and sleep with mates. In reality, all teenagers should take responsibility. It is crucial to find a compromise between offering adequate direction and having great independence to help prepare your teen for the future.

Show the Teen How Much Independence It Is Possible to Deal With

When your teen proves he can make smart decisions, you are going to give more independence. Whether you leave home late at night or if he goes out with his friends, remind him to deal with other things. Where do you go? Ask, "If your friend offered you a cigar, what should you do?" or "If someone rang the doorbell and said that he was an investigator to visit, why would you do it?" What should you do? Tell us sometimes that we are all wrong. Always be responsible for these errors. Tell your young person that he is not able to take further pressure if he tries to cover up his mistakes by pretending or denying his flaws.

Build Your Teen's Routine

Many teenagers have a lot to do and need some help to take responsibility for time management. Speak on how long he would spend studying, doing assignments, and doing extracurricular activities. Tell him how he will develop his best plan. While some teens may want to do some homework right after school, someone will want a break before they go back to college. He might consider an app or an electronic diary, which would allow him to recall what he has to do. Looking at his failures as an excuse to fix problems, whether he forgets to do his homework, or needs to stay late to do his assignment. If he tries to build his timeline, he will teach his organizational skills in the world of adults.

Encourage Your Young Person to Support

Learn to send your teen in a way to the society. Volunteering in an animal shelter, taking part in community-cleaning, or fundraising activities for a good cause may encourage your teenage boy to take a more responsible attitude. Sharing to the group will allow the young person to realize that it has the potential to improve the lives of people. It should help him become a responsible person who is committed to addressing and supporting others.

Teach the Qualities of Survival

The teen can be quickly believed to be on the road to success because he excels on the football field or completes homework on time. This does not mean that the young adult can embrace the burdens of the real world if he does well in certain aspects of his life. Try to ensure that you spend time training your teenage skills. It is important to have hands-on skills, like washing and cooking meals. Along with that, it is also necessary to ensure that your teen can handle his money and interact easily with others. While your teen can pick up some of these skills through staring at you, or by observation. You should know how to run a home and tackle real-life challenges successfully to your child.

Stay Mindful of Outcomes

Perhaps your adolescent can make mistakes (or even break the rules deliberately). Make sure his bad decisions have a negative effect. Efficient teachers may have rational implications, such as a lack of privileges. Always remove the need to apologies for your mistake or rescue the teens. The natural forces will also act as the most reliable warnings for the next time. It is painful to watch your child grow up and know that he will not ever be your son. However, if you do not instill a sense of duty, you are giving your teen a hardship. Your teen would thank you in the long run for making him into a confident and responsible person.

Allocate Age-Specific Tasks
Everybody in your house will have different duties to teach them. School going students should wash their hands with soap. Older children can be able to help remove their laundry machine, clean or set a dining table.

Put Off the Obligations of Each Family Member
You will now move over your new duty. Yet the two-year-old will also be one of the tiny assistants. Determine the roles of each family member in advance such that everyone is on the same page. Both mother and dad should take part in chore charts and weekly routines, and the entire family should know all that is to be done to run the household smoothly.

Praise Them for Keeping on Duties
We also fail to add gratitude for any situation that children perform, as we do not get the same recognition any time, we clean a kitchen counter or clear the lint trap of the dryer. Even when the children understand what their duty is, we need to make aware that we are there to applaud them for the hard work as they gather their clothes up off the ground and vacuum their belongings. We also fail to congratulate the children for any job at any time we dry up a kitchen counter or clear the lint trap of the dryer. Even the children know what duty rests with us, we need to be confident of our presence to pick up our garments from the

floor and to dust their furnishings for decent work.

Avoid Regular Recompenses

Each time you mop, are you having free ice cream? Try to teach a healthy boy. Let your child enjoy the pride of taking responsibility without having to be bribed instead of offering a candy bar if it collects the garbage. One day a week, you can treat your children with treats or reward them but do not bring a candy pocket, and you can get a slice out each time your children do something.

Wisely Using Compensation Tools

You can use too many resources to explain tasks, recognize certain milestones and strive for a goal or an incentive without having to walk beyond bribing and giving your child something that you described as his role in your household every day. Look for the household maps. Many children in your house have room in one place so that you do not need to buy different charts for every child. You should also draw the blanks on with the included dry-erase design so that you can personalize the duties in your drawing. When they have accomplished their task, every child gets a color star in the box, and at the very top, they describe the goal to be at until they perform all the tasks.

Let Your Children Feel Responsible for the Consequences

What if you quit house cleaning, brought the children anywhere, or brushed their teeth again? You must, of course, perform your duties and will always make sure that your children do so. We strive to push our children to do so-some work and other things that we have so frequently put out, but they seem to forget about them. There are other obligations. Let her know what the implications will be when you decide to layout your child's responsibilities. You are willing to do so as a lasting result, for instance, that inability to meet these five obligations leads to a loss of TV each week, or this can be calculated regularly based on your activities.

Enable a Step Forward

We know if we run away from our obligations, and our children still do not want to forget their duties. If your child does not want to understand you or neglect you, it can be unbelievably upsetting. Here, a step back is necessary. Do not lose your coolness and yell about the importance of your duties. You see them being responsive, not distrustful.

Be Persistent

Your children will need time to learn their duties. They are only young, and it will take time for them to learn and truly understand their responsibilities. When you want to raise a good kid, who is a respectful adult, your advice is vital.

Nonetheless, it has to be achieved in a manner that supports and makes them passionate about participating. Perhaps your child would continue to see expectations rather than something that is genuinely satisfying. Choose your priorities and note that raising a healthy child is a long-term task, which cannot be accomplished immediately.

Train the Kid with the Promise That We Will Always Purify Our Entire Messes

If you are optimistic and polite about it, he can understand it more efficiently and remember not to ponder over spilled milk. Encourage him to help, even though it is easier for him to do by handing him a sponge. He may like to help to tidy up and make it easier, as long as you are not criticizing it, and he is not territorial. When your little one is leaking her milk, say, "Milk is spilled, oops. It is all right; we will clean up."

If your schoolboy leaves his shoes littered in your direction, ask him to put them in a proper place. You will do so, anyway, before they leave your house when kids are always mindful of the high expectation that we will just wipe up our messes. Do not worry, and I am going to help. There are towels of the paper for you. I am going to find a sponge. They are all simpler, so happier throughout the universe.

Children Deserve a Chance to Help the Betterment

Find those forms and reflect on them even though you just note that he is kind to his younger brother, or you love singing like he often does. Any conduct you accept is going to expand. With the aging of your children, contributions both inside and outside the household can increase accordingly. Children will have two forms of responsibility: self-care and support for the well-being of the family. Evidence suggests that children who assist around the house are more likely to help with other circumstances than children who engage with self-care literally. You cannot expect them to be successful immediately, of course. It helps to raise accountability in age-specific ways continuously. Invite girls, three years old, to place their servings on the table. Note again that you invite your child to motivate him not to suspect or pressurize him.

Note No Child Wants to Do "Tasks" In His Right Mind

Your purpose is not to do a particular work, but to create a kid who would be able to contribute and take on responsibilities. Job is Fun. It is a nice thing to do the job. Give the structure, help, and assistance him that you need, including sitting with him and assisting him, if necessary, for the first thirty occasions. Keep in mind that it is going to be a lot more complicated than you do. You should know that these jobs are a delight and express with you the happiness of a successful career. He will finally perform these things too. If he loves them, the day will come even quicker.

Also, Have Them, Even If More Work Is for You, "Do It Myself" And "Support"

Nonetheless, children seek to conquer their physical environments, and while we help them to do so, they must be good. You interact with your child to help him find that the effort is acceptable. That is more important than doing the job quickly or correctly. They do remember that the bond, which motivates children to continue to participate. Adopt healthy activities to teach your children.

Seek to Ask Your Child to Consider More Than Just Send Orders

You could say, "What else do you need to do next to get ready for school?" The aim is to keep them in mind morning after morning before they internalize it and begin handling their daily activities. For example, to the dallying child in the regular, rather than shouting, "Brush your teeth! Is your bag packed? Do not forget your lunch!" you could say.

Provide Schedules and Layout

They are critical in the lives of youngsters, not least because they give them the ability to handle themselves in a variety of activities that are not incredibly motivating. They first clean the bed, vacuum the toys, and get ready in the morning.

Then they develop positive research and treatment procedures. Eventually, when rehearsing domestic activities such as cleaning or preparing easy meals, they learn essential life skills.

Prepare to Make Your Kid Accountable for Your Experiences

Do not ask him to apologize if your son hurt the feelings of his little brother. It is not going to say anything, so it is not going to help him. Firstly, guess his thoughts and help him uncover the entangled emotions that snarled him. So, ask him what he can do to change both of them as soon as he feels better. Perhaps he will be able to explain. But maybe It is going to feel like missing his nose, so he is more comfortable to mend things by reading a story or helping him to set the menu, or to hold him. Since you are not required to do so, he will opt to restore, which makes him feel comfortable and will make him regain more likely. It comes about the chip on your back. The child behaves like the one getting damaged or insulted and is not ready to continue fixing, so he behaves like it is inevitable to execute his acts. It is a significant health initiative you are going to need to invest in, so begin today by creating trust, listening to the concerns of your child, and remembering the old feelings. It is the former reparation.

Help Your Child in Compensation for Items Lost

Children help to care for missing library books and tablets, shattered windows, or equipment left out to rust from their budget; there are small risks of repeated infringements.

Do Not Even Try to Save Your Kid from a Tough Situation

Help him sort through his thoughts and worries to make sure he does not only avoid the challenge but help him address the issue himself. No matter it involves apologies or more precise adjustment.

The Obligation for the Concept and Responsibilities

Be clear about the right choices that are taken. Hold the promises to your kid, and do not apologize. This sign states space is designated for those with physical disabilities. Why will he take the risk of keeping his promises and commitments with you if you do not follow through on picking up the notebook he wants for homework or playing the game with it on Saturday?

Do Not Name Your Kid "Irresponsible"

Never name your child "irresponsible," because the way we treat our children is still a promise that fulfills itself. Instead, show him the skills he needs to carry out. For instance, if he always loses things, teach him to stop every time he leaves his friend's house or any other place and check the things.

Educate Your Children to Plan in Writing

Start at middle school on weekends or before, if your life is crazy. Take only a sheet of paper, list your child's time on the left, and ask what he will need this weekend. Put the game of cricket, the lesson of guitar, the birthday party and all the science project move – content store, volcano construction, printing, and writing the definition. Be sure to block downtime — go for daddy ice cream, relax and hear music. Most children feel that their stress level remains weak, as they know when It is all over. It helps you most of all, to control your time and be responsible for your obligations.

Every Child Need the Payroll Exposure

Every child needs payroll training, which gives them exact responsibilities in the real world. Start by asking your eight-year-old to do things that you would usually not expect from him (wash your house, weed the garden), and then inspire him to grow into disgusting jobs in the community. Few conditions are as strong as transparency in the work system outside the home.

Establish a Household without Fault:

We just like to blame others immediately if things go wrong. It is like resolving fault that will keep the issue aside from repeating, or cancels our responsibility. Blaming others makes him protective rather than amending, the child is more likely to watch his back and to strike. This thing is the number one reason why children lie to their parents. Worse still, if we blame them, children find all sorts of excuses why it was not their fault at least in their minds, so they are less likely and more likely to replicate the incident. Blaming the true love is reverse. Why are we doing so, then? To make us feel less out of reach and to believe that we played a role in the case, although small, as well. The next time you want to accuse others, refrain. You just embrace the situation. From an appropriate location, you will still consider more options than a fault.

Teach Child Be the One Who They Are

Surveys suggest that people who embrace accountability are individuals who can vary and stand out in a given situation. You want to raise this kind of kid. Allow your children to do the things that they want to do. Ask them what thing inspires you and what kind of activities you want to do in your spare time. Never compare your children in front of others and in front of their siblings too.

CHAPTER 3: PREPARE YOUR KID FOR SUCCESS

The growing parent would like to bring their children to the complete, healthy, and prosperous life that they can lead. We are what we do again and again," Aristotle wrote, "Excellence is not an act, then, but an attitude." How we talk to our children is real. We recently discussed how wealthy parents carry an enormous benefit to their children, only by getting them into more affluent communities. Not every reader loved that suggestion. Others on social media called it a formula for snobby or insecurity. All right, fair enough. Leave that away, and then reflect on seven essential things that nearly all parents can do to give their children more edge every day. It is almost a universal rule that parents want a better future for their kids than they had. One of the easiest ways to make your child succeed is to encourage safe lifestyles. We are also aware that wellness-centered children often grow to be more reliable, happy, and more successful adults, contributing to success. Food plays an essential role as it can heal or damage strength, mood, concentration, and more. Let us be clear: if you are lenient, irritable, nervous, and bubbly, you simply cannot be gratified.

Let Your Children Do Their Work
Take the trash off, rip the grass, do wash the dishes not only ways of simplifying your life, but also means of enhancing your children's lives.

Educate the Moral Competences
Have you ever been interacting with emotionally awkward people? You certainly would not be shocked to hear that children with strong social skills were more productive then. Socially skilled childcare has a much better opportunity to graduate in high school and have full-time jobs by age 25. Then children with poor social skills, who may communicate with their friends without motivation, support others to appreciate their thoughts and fix their problems.

Teach Strong Educational Aspirations and Give Them
Two activities are mixed, but they have little to do with them. First, if you want your children to go to kindergarten, make sure that you set early as a successful example. In the meantime, you would always need them to study at work. Parents who watched college in the future of their

child appeared to be controlling their child for this reason instead of income and other capital sources.

Learn to Establish Good Ties

We also learned that the parents who struggled in marriage but rather who opted to live together for their children's sake. That may be impressive, but it is more important for any parent and siblings to be in close touch. Firstly, a study found that children are more relevant to grow up in a house that has no tension between their parents, and secondly, children who, in their first three years, were given 'intensive treatment' had stronger ties at school. They had more good connections and academic success in the 30s.

Excite Them for Math

It is essential to read young children, but also to teach them mathematics skills. Advanced math skills were transformed into economic, scientific success in a survey of 35,000 young children. Most children do not want to learn mathematics skills and do not like this subject. Arrange different tasks and games to teach mathematical skills to your child.

Prepare to Test Them. And Do Not Hate Failure

You had heard about taking a growth attitude toward a fixed or scarce perspective. You want a development philosophy for your children. You do not want to see loss, which happens to all of us, as an opportunity to improve and grow, not as an end. Do not worry; in other words. Moreover, consider controlling the stress level or, at least, managing the severity of the tension. Gain and loss are part of life. Teach your child never to lose hope in case of a failure.

Present Job Ethics and Success
If you want to have specific behavior of your children, ethical behavior is probably the most likely way to do so. (The second most effective approach might be to model bad behavior and encourage it to benefit from your actions, but I am going to recommend the first idea.) A report indicates that children who grow up with working moms benefit from those who do not. The study showed that working mother's sons had been to school for longer, had more workplace control, and received more income 23 percent more than their fellow students, who were nurtured by home mothers."

Establish a Relationship on Learning
The reality is that it is better to see the relationship between you and the teachers of your child when it comes to teaching your children. When it comes to teaching your children, take the opportunity to work closely with them, and make sure they fulfill the needs of your child and make the best of their educational experiences. Invest in their studies.

Render Life-Long Learning a Priority

It is a learning experience, and those who know early in life that we always have chances to learn and develop are well prepared for success. Education can never begin or be finished in the classroom. Build an atmosphere in which your child will spread a love of knowledge and global curiosity.

Promote the Interests

The best and most successful men in life are not always the most money-makers. Instead, you also find the things you truly want and enjoy in your life. A way had been discovered to make it an essential part of your life. Whether as a career or a hobby, inspire your kids to explore the world around them. Early to find something that inspires them, so embrace them to encourage them to pursue their interests.

Incorporate the Importance of Lasting Relationships

Strong social ties can be indispensable early in life. Allow your child to understand the importance that strong friendships create and develop first in life. It lets them realize how important it is to have a good support network to pursue new opportunities, meet barriers, resolve problems, and take advantage of life.

No Fear from Failure

In life, we stop doing anything different, and potentially excellent because we are scared that we are not good at it. This thing can be a unique way to skip success and joy in life. Then tell your kids that it is all right to lose. Life is a game of trial and error, and it is the only way you can ever learn is to test your limits, venture beyond your comfort zones and be comfortable with the thoughts of potentially useless things.

Know About Future

Many people are successful at pushing off things they do not want to tackle, even when they are too late. If we like it or not, we all have the potential, and it is most likely that those who intend to do it as early as possible will be prepared for a lot of failures and build a positive growth strategy.

While it is difficult to guarantee our children happiness, as parents, we are committed to helping our children achieve. Using the tips to boost your children as they learn, develop, evolve, and make them better to achieve their life objectives.

Success and Dignity in Confidence

It was not so long ago that accomplishment made people happy, but it is now recognized that joy increases the likelihood of achievement. Good people are more likely to strive for ambitions, to pursue their opportunities, and inspire others with enthusiasm and excitement.

It not only decreases depression and increases coping skills, leading to more excellent health and a more successful employee; it also helps to avoid other kinds of illnesses like cancer. Junk food, smoking, and quality time are three positive activities that people do every day. We need to be careful with not just absence. It is known to be much more expensive than the absence of other workers.

Healthy Child=Healthy Adults

The parents and guardians have a vital role to play as they provide standards of right, life-long decisions for children. Support your child by the following:

Promote a Good Weight

Malnutrition, obesity, and other forms are both of the associated chronic illnesses such as diabetes and fatty liver syndrome, which have a significant physical and emotional impact. Overweight is potentially one of the three preventable premature mortality risk factors.

Do not presume that your child has health issues. Comfortably due to age; obesity places children at higher risk of type 2 diabetes, elevated cholesterol, metabolic syndrome as well as other illnesses. (The only two avoidable causes are smoking and high blood pressure). Encourage them, instead of waiting before TV and video games, to engage in after-school events. When they are having dinner, let your child enjoy a salad or chopped vegetables. This is no problem as you should add more fruit and vegetables to your diet with a little imagination rather than potato chips and cookies. Please note that the mind needs as much stimulation as the body, thereby cultivating play, puzzles, chat, and physical activity.

Offer Them Your Garden
It does not depend if it is a strip of land in the backyard or front yard, a fire escape container garden or an avocado pit in a glass of water, children are interested so that they enjoy everything where they grow up.

They will have to cultivate, and from the start, to finish, they will take care of something. Additional skills, such as hand-eye coordination, counting, and calculation, will also be developed. We will know the ever-important ability and persistence. Members who are not cautious would be short-lived in their professions.

Participation of a Fitness Plan in the Neighborhood
For example, wellness at schools, which encourages healthy food, environmental awareness, and exercise in general for children, tackles childhood obesity in particular. Encourage your child to participate in different games and exercises to make their bodies in shape. A healthy body has a healthy mind.

Important communication skills for children

As parents, we affect our children with what we do, what we value and neglect, how we spend time with our children, and what we encourage. Your children will develop a variety of things in their everyday life that will serve them well for the rest of their lives.

Writing and Reading

Writing and reading produce language, encourages critical and imaginative thought, improves communication skills, and thus foster empathy and compassion, which are essential qualities of leadership.

Reading

The 21st century needs good reading and writing skills. The basis for lifelong reading starts with oral text, which provides the children with new ideas and encourages enthusiasm and imagination. Reading activates the brain and is more neurobiological than repetitive activities such as watching TV and hearing music. You have got more time to reflect while you listen. You will read a particular pause to learn and comprehend learning.

Writing

The process of papering increases self-expression and fosters creativity. Some scholars find writing as inciting the absorption, encoding, storing, and retrieval of knowledge of the brain to understand the principles of mathematics and science. Teach the children to enjoy reading and learning and writing as a blessing for the rest of their life and the desired profession. In the challenges and competitions that your child will face as an adult, you will give him great benefit by promoting reading and writing.

Communication

The willingness to exchange ideas, emotions, and knowledge becomes essential as the world has become more interconnected and interdependent. Productive adult and social communication skills make it possible for your child to accomplish the things they need from life. However, few parents actively advocate strong communication skills, especially useful when communicating to groups or general audiences, because of the apparent benefits of this ability. Nevertheless, parents should do a few specific things to help their children become effective communicators:

Promotes Correct Pronouncement

Words share concepts and create verbal images. Uttering words, in particular, repeated mispronounced words create false expectations and harm the identity of your child.

Enhance Vocabulary

Out of some 470,000 English entries, the average adult American knows about 20,000 words. But in conversations, it uses just about 3000 a day. The more words your kid learns and uses, the more they can connect. Speaking aloud and using words to inspire children and adults is a healthy way to develop vocabulary.

Train to Talk to Other People

Some adults are scared that they should meet a community and speak, while the majority of children prefer to be the target. The early learning of the ability to communicate with others is a life-long advantage.

Bilingualism Approach

Early learning of a second language provides a variety of benefits, including the actual rise in grey matter density of the brain. The frequency of grey matter is related to vocabulary, memory, and focus. Human brain development is influenced by the second language learning experience. Scientific research has enhanced the bilingual children significantly who outperform their peers who speak a single language. The incomprehension, intellectual intelligence, and emotional discernment assessments where the universe is understandable, it brings considerable professional and social opportunities that do not enable a person who is restricted to American English to converse with other countries in their mother tongue, especially where goods are manufactured and sold. And, most of all, it is easy for your infant to learn another language, and because of his greater neural and cognitive "plasticity," It is easy for them to understand.

Social Confidence

The benefits of adult physical education are known for decades. In one study, after the other, gross and fine muscles have adapted to carry out every day work, have a positive effect on future obesity in late years, and exercise mental stimulation.

The majority of specialists suggest children invest at least 60 minutes a day in a fair play and work with at least two hours a day. It is much less important how good your children are in sports than just going out and watching them. Families will allow their children to play numerous recreational games and activities, including golf, soccer, swimming, and those including collective efforts such as baseball, basketball, volleyball, and football.

The challenge of parents focused on height, physical dominance, and aggression is exceptional and may lead to constant, diminishing injuries. Football for secondary and high schools, though, it is particularly common due to its social advantages.

When your child can play football, allow it to partake in other off-season sports and ensure that the team has adequate professional attention and regular trainers. Tennis and golf are two life-long activities, giving both athletic advantage and daily social contact. They are also beneficial to the following function. A new report states that the golfers earn a lot more than non-golfers and pay extra for golfing skills.

Music Skills
While music is long regarded as an emotional experience, yet we do not know how sounds are treated in the brain and why music lasts for so long in our memories. Yet we know that it is useful to listen to music and learn to play a musical instrument in helping children with

physical pain, with cognitive or compartmental disorders or with low focus.

Studies on the influence of music on college and pre-school children have identified many trends: Participating in music and movement programs leads to improving positive social and emotional skills for adolescents. Also, music lessons for a single year will have a lasting effect on brain functions.

- Lowest drug use was recorded by high school students participating with bands and orchestras.
- Students in high school education have higher verbal and math scores than their classmates on the SAT.
- The most popular group of college graduates accepted by medical schools are music students at college.

There are many benefits for adults: music listening, music performance, or instrumentation can relieve stress and sadness.

There are many different benefits for adolescents. The music of older people with Alzheimer's disease, illnesses, chronic pain, stroke, and depression is commonly used. Introduce the kids to the love of music early so that they can enjoy it throughout life. We wonder if we can secure them when we're not about to get packed. We may not be in a position to plan our children's future, but at least our children should be preparing for our future.

Keep Up with Them

This activity can be annoying, and you often believe the sentences go to and fro. Contrary to that, the researchers found that parents who express strong aspirations continue to be effective in children, and escape main pitfalls.

A survey of 15,000 girls aged 13-14 and 23-24 over ten years has clearly shown that those who have reliably exhibited strong child aspirations were the children who did not want to hear all the "high demands," and they never responded to them adequately.

Give Them Appropriate Acknowledgement

Families honor their children in two significant respects.

1) Innate appreciation of skills: fantastic work! Examples: You are so intelligent. You are so smart!

2) Lobbying effort: Fantastic work! You have been practicing and making things out!

If you thank me for my inborn personality, you applaud me for:

a) something I have nothing to do with accomplishing.

b) something I cannot control.

Yet if you thank me for my commitment, you help me to build the muscles that I want to develop correctly. If you are a new parent, while your children are older, you find that this difference matters most. The infants as young as 1 to 3 years old can be quantified by the results of these reward techniques.

Bring Them Out
When the weather is clear for both kids and you, it is always entertaining. Discuss that. Bring your child for an outing to enjoy the weather, and then, for six or seven hours, what do we want our children to do? Sit in classrooms. Instead, science suggests that you can allow children to play outdoors.

The Strength of Talking with Kids
We also communicate clearly and implicitly with our family. Do not wait to talk on serious issues. We will be late. Truly excellent work! The trick, though, is to hold discussions back and forth.

In the test, 36 children using FMRI were tested by experts to assess how the brain reacts to different kinds of communication. Researchers observed that in children having in backward conversations, the field of Boca, which focuses on speech development and language learning, became even more successful.

In language tests, syntax and verbal thinking skills, children with more significant activity in the area, scored higher in the brain. The profound revolutionary feature of our paper is that it first reveals the family interactions in the home, which is linked to child brain development. This is almost amazing how parenting seems to affect the growth of the brain biologically.

Recall the Difference (Word)

The vocabulary and cognitive ability of children from higher-income families were much higher, and it has been estimated that the children have been subjected to nearly 30,000,000 more words in life in contrast with the children in the lower-income families for the first years. Yet the results of this new analysis show that "thirty million words of distance" are not all that has collapsed. The conversational turn-over is the same, regardless of the socio-economic position. Children from lower earnings households or parental schooling have the same opportunities as conversational turn-over groups. They prefer to take part in conversational turn-over.

Factual Talk

The argument is not that the children should have profound intellectual discussions, but rather they should have conversations that require reflective dialogues. This thing is not a daunting jump, and in the long term, they will gain significantly; engaging experiences tend to improve communication skills in general, and this is a prerequisite for advancement with any further profession. After all, the discussion may not be so cheap when it comes to your child's success.

It is not astonishing that most of the boys are young, loud, wild, and rugged. We have ideas to keep them safe when kids become adults, and you lose your patience. Many of us dream that kids are looking happily at books or putting blocks together to create a tower before becoming adults. Of course, we soon remember that children can be energetic because we are adults, so boys are typically more energetic and violent than girls. Though there are still exceptions, not every boy has the same actions or can be bound to the same gender roles. Parenting boys can be a handful more often. We have ideas for parents that can assist you with parenting boys at the edge of their heads.

You do appreciate their deviations from your children as a mother of sons. However, what do you think about these differences? How do you teach your children to be responsible and open? We should make the world more friendly towards children, particularly in kindergarten. If you are premature and fleeting, you have to turn your children into good people, loyal, and to obey us. In countries with children beginning kindergarten at six or seven, they do even better. Many young people, but especially those active boys, who need it well, play and are busy. That is just the edge.

Kids may not have exposure to the developmental stages. One is the 'absolute four' who bring puberty hormones well outside their bodies while hormones are attacked. As I write in my book that includes so many Irish mothers and fathers around the world, I immediately knew what I was writing. Children under four have high levels of rotation, rumbling, and perturbation.

To know it is not vain but rather a blessing. (While a sudden change in behavior is worth going to the bottom of something is terrible). But young boys (and a few girls) are most typically eager to get out, which means that we have to figure out how to do it much as they would do if we were a sheepdog in the house.

You can go up, stroll, and visit other areas. You can help to learn how to handle the brakes gently, but quickly. We trigger confusion as we consider a child terrible because he is a boy, which typically results in anger and the beginning of a poor guy. You must set limitations and advise him to rest; do it kindly, please.

Another period of infancy called adrenal arches just last year was noticed in a long-term survey of 1,200 children reaching the twenties. Around the age of 8 or 9, adrenal arches begin. The number of hormones known as sugar hormones was growing. Since it is typically described as the emotional eight, he is as confused as you are. He is lost. Initial puberty stirrings are adrenal arches, but no significant signs exist for three or four years.

Many boys wind up more strongly than girls. Now all the girls and women are so different. You will never be able to kick, kill, threaten, or even treat them poorly. The emotional cycle corresponds mostly with puberty, which is typically two years longer than for infants and around 14 before they reach maximum elevation with becoming fully fertile. Children cannot grow up or sophisticate at 16 or 17 years.

Many males, though, are bigger or heavier than girls and thus stronger than their mates. It is a warning to the girls or women, sisters, or brothers, to never beat them or even to hurt them is completely necessary. Fathers and mothers will reaffirm this message together, live with them, and remember the right person and wait for nothing. A kid wants to learn what it is (see what is meant by those he is growing up with) to make him enjoyable.

Train your son to live the same way when they are young to know the correct way to perform to handle them like they are older when they were young. Elevating children is not easy. It is challenging to know the right way simply because our kids do not have a map. My problem is I am a father of a twin boy. I hope cognitive and behavioral research will help us in bringing up a child differently. We cannot always get everything right as parents, but we are trying to do everything we know we can work with them every day. For raising the youth, there are seven main concepts. The following are:

Confrontational Supervising

This may be disturbing whether a boy is drawn to gaming guns or violent video games, but the kid sees violence as a fantasy to save the world, as a kid who pretends to kill an evil individual. Typing extreme imagination play whether they are cops, robbers, or zombie apocalypse can help kids get right and wrong.

Furthermore, partnerships and self-confidence also encourage such sports. He is going to leave the game if a friend of your kid finds the play too hard.

If you note the disappointment of your kid, take the time to add empathy and try to consider the emotions of other people.

Furthermore, rough and tumble rivalry for kids during the entire childhood is natural. For older children, discussions about why you are not happy with a particular form of play or video game will lead to a meaningful conversation about the principles of your family. Your children may come as a shock to you with the sophisticated descriptions of their play.

Pattern Ethical Actions

It is essential to stay calm even when you are worried about aggressive actions. Exploited violence toward their violent actions is something that parents can discourage. While at present, an extreme or serious illness may interrupt the action, heavily disciplined children are more likely to be violent in the long run. Design respectful conduct, and make sure you applaud them. Sit back and ask them about their desires, like bugs or robots. To compliment your children, whether they acquire insect awareness or take care of their cherished toys.

Enhance Infancy and Awareness

Boys are not constructed from slugs, snails, and puppy-dog tails, in light of the classic nursery rhyme. Explain the value of goodness by swapping toys with friends and being compassionate with pets to grow your son's more sensitive side.

You can also read historical people who promote unity and equality. Discuss the unprecedented energy of the boxer, "Muhammad Ali," while still fighting for social justice or how Martin Luther King, Jr., had led non-violent and robust civil rights demonstrators. Find ways in your son's life to establish successful male role models. Make appointments with fathers, parents, uncles, and grandpas, or engage in volunteer service mentorships. A young boy can feel happier by expressing kindness and caring as though nothing is wrong.

Promoting Emotional Speech

Boys can be better at thinking about their emotions because they take an active part in recognizing their emotional side. Exploring a passion may reduce the probability of an emotional reaction and disseminate exacerbations. Family men can help him appreciate the feelings of a young boy's life by teaching constructive ways to convey emotions. It may take a while for boys to become tolerant and willing to talk about their thoughts and feelings. If it is clear that something is wrong, but your son does not want to talk, hold him away from pressing and stop by asking him questions. Just hug him instead and let him know when he is about to speak that you will be there.

Look at the Dust and Sound

The area across the bath may be darker than ever, but sometimes letting things go is the only way for a change of mind.

Note that it washes mud, but it can take years to recall memories of enjoyable games.

At some point along the way, I realized that I could torment myself and my boys by trying to keep things together. I could relax and let us all enjoy a little more. Though the play is fun and children are happy, pants will fix the majority of mud problems. When it comes to noise, pick a place at home. Build playgrounds in a converted basement or use the bedroom away from common space. However, if you still cannot cope with a high decibel, take your children to a playground nearby or the park and let them relax, yell, yell, and unleash their steam. Everybody should return to the home kitchen to have a sweet, well-deserved snack after a stint of running and rude behavior.

Know on Valuation
Your conviction determines how you teach your family. Consider the standards behind all parenting practices as the fundamental base. Our values influence our parenthood in every area.

Therefore, thinking about our values is very necessary. Firstly, it would impact how your child learns to value others because you want to treat people as you wish. However, this also influences how you teach your child to take care of others because, first of all, you love yourself.

A kid motivated to value others because they can share their toys with their friends, and they know that they want to share this condition with others. Their coworkers are more interested in sharing their toys. A child motivated to first think of himself becomes less likely to share, as he has noticed that it is more valuable to have the gift than to share it because it is better than others. Always know your heart and values while ultimately educating your kids. If your child is trained as a reliable moral person with strong beliefs, these tips are just beneficial. Their acts must be regulated by the foundation of ethical values and a sense of justice. It is the base of all other skills.

Offer the Way to Your Authority

Acknowledge how aggressive and thrilling your boys are than your girls. Instead of draining your money, turn it into something constructive. Boys need more attention than girls. Keep your attention all the time on your boys.

Remember How Frustration for Turnaround

Life is an attribute of downfall. When a man struggles to succeed, his talent will influence him in the long run. If a man is drained and cannot pick him up after a defeat to continue again, he never gets there. When people are motivated during their youth to unite and start again, they learn how to avoid loss.

This thing is a good thing to say that your son should try again. The effort and outcome should be illustrated. In the beginning, if you train your son to ride a bike, your boy will fall down several times until he learns his skills. You encourage them to get up and do it. Do not worry about the outcome that lies alone on a bike. Thanks to more for working hard and getting up and trying again. Thank you. After a significant attempt, they can eventually excel in cycling. You will always praise them so they will learn, but once again, make sure that they do not shine with their hard work and perseverance. It is essential to achieve in time, effort, and resources. The best way to build a mindset that benefit is to raise anxiety about the outcome. E.g., if you rely on the result to win a game, you feel lost when you have got a loss. We will now see how we would improve if you can play the game and appreciate your hard work and constructive actions. We will get up and continue again, but they do not seem like a complete disaster. You can see the value of their health practice and an original attitude that can be modified.

Take Control of Your Mood
Always recognize that many terrifying threats in this universe can hurt the hearts of the people. The risks must be handled vigorously, public violence should be avoided, and symptoms of pain, abduction, or exhaustion should be detected.

Try to Hold the Closer You Can
Keep your sons in contact with each other. Hold free touch, leadership, and holy discipline. Children are a distinct resemblance to their parents. Both time and quantity, I like both mother and father. In fact, according to the

increase in the number of single mothers, certain factors are not sustainable. The studies also have shown that single mothers bring up boys well as a model for boys. If the father cannot reveal himself, the next best thing is the good father, who has a positive influence on the life of the boy. Children with single moms have considerably lower moral values in comparison to children in traditional households where both the mum and their rear dad are substantially weaker and more aggressive comparatively.

All hope is not lost for single mothers. Our daily research showed that having a father or mother in a child's life allows the infant to develop its schooling.

It is less likely that they will be prevented, less likely to become addicted to drugs, or have greater confidence and self-esteem. That supports enormously young people. They should not be taken lightly. Our children need strong male role models and a parent to help them develop and flourish in their lives.

If a father is not in the picture, a brother, uncle, or family member will fill the vacuum instead. Strong role models are essential because they can mold life. Children need to spend time with a parental adult, or an influential male figure, finding and educating and inspiring them to be good people.

BE Your Boy's Hero

Give your children positive role models. Always seek to spend time with a close family member or friend if your father is not at home. Invite or visit those friends or relatives who are the most favorite personalities of your child.

Give the Right Time

Give each other and your children a lot of time. You can adjust your schedule, but give time and material to your children. Giving them time also takes the form of real love and devotion. Some people believe that with embrace or affection, a boy can become weak. This thing is not valid. "I love you" is a mentality that makes you better boyfriends, moms, mothers and role models as adults. It also offers significant benefits such as physical well-being, reduced anxiety, better coordination, increased satisfaction, and reduced stress in health care. Many clinicians recommend at least 12 improvement snacks a day, while others suggest as the highest number of treats possible and give improved outcomes daily.

The inquiry is for girls and women. Everyone deserves to love and be in touch with each other. Everyone needs love and affection. Hugging is a vital way for parents to enjoy our children happily every day. Our children tend to be affectionate based on their home experiences. You might feel awkward as an adult if you were born in a family that never received any cuddle. Let her know that her love is kind, and every day let her use these kisses. Make use of this as your routine of continually picking up your son and telling, "I love you."

Their Desires Are Served By

The purpose of man-bash in our culture is to offset by reinforcing manhood, and the value of a child as a person.

Living without dreams is a future without hopes. Before they try to pursue them, do not pinch your goals. Your child may aspire to be a professional footballer, for example, as an adult. There can be optimism and dream. They are 14, and they want to stay happy and healthy. Most parents wanted to avoid these dreams. There is a small possibility that you will become a professional athlete like a footballer; however, you should not. With time you need to know that you are good enough to sail from your sports participation to the next level. That is why it is essential to make your child well-rounded. You cannot put all the eggs in the same nest, as the old saying suggests. Instead, you should understand the importance of other sports, and the school should do a lot of research, so you never know that you would not always be left out of the event. Even if it seems like a kid tries their desires one in a million bullets, they get valuable life lessons. You learn how to work hard, and the only thing you think of is what it takes.

In reality, nothing is simple. If that's the dream, let them do it (not sell your house to fund the project). Enable them to draw fuel from the rocket. We will see what it takes for us to do so. It is okay if you do not achieve this goal too. It is fascinating to know what they discovered along the trip. For starters, as a football player, we learned about teamwork, physical fitness, preparation, and commitment. You cannot become a pro football player, but you will learn the facts over time. A parent does not like reality to smash expectations. Enable children to hope and dream, for that is what makes them suffer hardest.

Positive lessons to learn from learning are incentives to work hard even with deceit. You should not stop them from seeking a goal if they are afraid of being ashamed. Failure and a determination to get up after a setback makes them influential people.

A Foster Faith
Make your children's spiritual development. Your focus on parenting is motivating them to have a connection to God.

Teach Skills of Good Player
Energetic sport is a significant learning talent. We cannot perform in class. Ultimately, everybody is going to lose. Some will find it impossible to do so. Parents should teach their young children this skill. In the beginning, you should not sulk but congratulate your boy while playing board games and your son loses. Starting young is a smart idea if you have played, verbally.

It is more fun to be a successful athlete as a young teen or an adult if you have met other champions down the road. The regulated activities mentioned by Children's Health are: Good sport does not appear to be a decision, but it describes qualities such as winning, valuing one's opponents, and losing with grace.

To Build the Ethical Workforce

Do not do this for them! Do not do it about them. Seek to educate the children with a strong working principle. While Mom did it every day for them, they are not going to learn to make a bunk. Accountability and excellent ethical standards are taught through daily experience. It must start at an early age. When the infant is three years old, it will help the daily tasks of the household, such as the collection of waste, toys sorting, feeding, and washing plates. You may not be doing the best job, but when you are young, you continue to be trained.

Give them vital life and parental awareness often by schooling. This helps you to grow a good work ethic. You will be growing up, and you should know that you should cast out the garbage before it is over like you have been doing for years to come.

Do not say that boys and girls have other household duties. Provide the girls and boys with all their skills. Cooking, brushing, and cleaning should be taught to the children. What will be happening to them when they are going to school or their first job? You have to develop skills to make yourself stronger. This allows them both a dream and a wonderful life. No one needs to marry a man who cannot work at all in the home.

You may be accused of not knowing your children, so it does not motivate you to find a decent wife if you do not learn how to indulge in homework. Getting a successful daughter and a successful wife means being able to do things such as laundry and cooking. That is not a safe way to teach others or prepare them for any potential relationship, to expect people to do so while their mums were growing up. If you just want to live alone, teach them good job ethics beyond your home, it ends with domestic chores.

Characteristics Learn in Dialogue

For every child's relationships and professions, communication skills are essential. Communication abilities are the foundations of all human beings. Relations and career ambitions can become easier to accomplish as they find it hard to communicate.

A study reports that technology is an important cause for many young people to lose strong listening skills. Your face-to-face communications are compromised in a world of ubiquitous email and instant messaging. There is so much time wasted without meaningful encounters face to face. The first step in improving strong communication skills is to minimize the access of your child to technologies and services. Speak every day to your child, and discussion helps to develop excellent communication skills.

If you have a young adult currently who has difficulty in acquiring excellent communication skills, it was not too late. We can still learn these skills, but we can grow better contact abilities in our lives. Sport is a means of handling youth. Sport has Effective touch on boys. By debate, these skills and open-ended questions can be learned through functional communication abilities for those of younger people. In this situation, you will laugh, applaud, and ask questions. This form of expression is an excellent way to teach children and encourage children to develop bonds today as well as in the future, both verbally and orally.

Frequently Engaging in Polycyclic and General Observations

It is not only a lesson for your son to show you a decent way. It is a day-to-day lesson for children. Take the time to use the proper mark and politeness every day in your home. Here is how you can motivate your son to be a man of integrity. This means that you can show them how they can eat socially from the moment you prepare for their meal. You will not grow things by natural means if you do not learn to exercise those things at home. Generosity, but still on the front of the job is essential in relationships. The study demonstrates that you need to practice in a suitable format for job development and referral letters. For example, if you agree that your son should appreciate and tolerate others even though they are not especially good for him, which will help him understand how to communicate with hard workers in the future. Your son will always have raw people in his life. It is essential to find meaningful ways to handle them in his life.

Encourage Him to Help Others

Compassion is what we all desire for our children. Your kindness for others will affect the climate. Not just your future partner, but also your future children, coworkers, and your friends. Learning to be kind to our children will change the climate. There are some practical ways of making your child kind:

• Put them to volunteer service

• Instruct them to express words of gratitude, genuine affection for others

• Do not push them to become a dictator

• Instruct them how to handle others with reverence as they are

• Teach them how to treat everyone you want them because they do

Skills Creation for Obstipation Determination

Pressure from the parents is somehow justified. Competition between pairs is a reality. It starts and even never stops in adulthood. We should encourage our children to do better and stick up for these options, particularly though their teacher wants to place pressure on them in other decisions. You need skills that illustrate how our children can be able to avoid it. It requires first teaching them to understand and stand up for their thoughts and beliefs. After that, then to teach them how to communicate their identity successfully under these conditions of social pressure.

By playing scenarios with your kids, you will encourage them to protect themselves and their choices. For starters, you can play a part in getting a suitable medication for your boy. First, experiment by telling you to say 'no' to drugs so you would trust the decision.

Enable you to trust your religion so that your choice can be made on a firm basis. If you do not think you should, your only reason may not be adequate because it is your closest friend who promises that you meet your closest friend. Then, warn them not to react violently. In this situation, for example, they find ways of saying it on their language, which is calm but trustworthy, such as no, I do not take any drugs, and I will not forfeit my right to college due to the lack of a substance regulation or the fact that the drugs trap me. Let him believe that it is smart to make choices to do better than his peers. We must learn how to be persistent in essential problems. The following advice is also really significant.

Explain the Healthy Lives Importance

They cannot make the right life decisions for their children until they know right from wrong. The lesson finishes in the form. If you wish better for your son, urge him to make any good potential choices without drugs, alcohol, minors, and pornography, which are seen as highly addictive and counteracting to a healthier development. What are not the only examples of parent's alcohol control vices? Although alcohol and drugs are the most prevalent in teenagers, video games, gambling, shopping, and the internet are all the causes that cause other addictions.

Every day should be tackled. For starters, to prevent game violence and not to give your children unlimited play should any of these problems are restricted. Always have average time restrictions for games and access to technology. Being involved in engaging gaming activities, and your son does not just stay on his time in the game every day. Support him to try other things, as he needs more than gaming interests and ambitions. Speak to your child about their choices about your life and how their decisions will affect the future. Next, a teen may believe that it is not appropriate to smoke pot.

You do not learn about the drug program zero-tolerance, for alcohol, at the college they expect to enter. The risks and drawbacks for teens of smoking pots are still nonsensical. Tackle main and even trivial issues. Have difficult talks before making bad decisions. A parent lists ways parents can help their children make the right decisions. In this respect, they can improve their sons. Enable them to see, however slight, the consequences of their choices. For example, you do not believe in the science of your kid. During the day of the science show, we are the only ones who will not have experience. You have not been asking for your assistance. This certainly was that you said they had a task to do the previous day. Your activities have consequences, and guardians have to help the children to consider the moral implications of their acts and decisions. When a mother feels terrible for her son because his study is not done, and when he sleeps the night before he leaves, so he discovers that his mother is there to save him when things get tough. He does not feel bad; he did not have a job and cannot compete at the trade show for technology. Since mom solves issues, he is not going to get a bad ranking. It is not supporting him in the long term. He needs to confront these vulnerabilities to understand the consequences of his acts and decisions. If a project does not complete, it will lead to a disaster, and he has deliberately opted that not to do the job in the period stated.

Teach Him to Be Honest

Dishonest and disappointed adults have a weak conscience. If you want your son to become a man of integrity, they must realize that honesty is unbelievably essential from a young age. Below are a couple of ways your child can be adopted.

- Prototype for Integrity.
- Do not tell white lies because children still have little lies to discern from big lies. Do not lie, because you are the only one that says the facts.

- Foster sincerity as you are not to be asked whether you think you need to be punished.
- Give your child a chance to tell the truth without pushing him.
- Do not expose dishonest children to ease their life. First of all, it makes you a cheat to say to them that you cannot go there today as the park is closed.
  Do not even lie to a better or more faithful life for your kids. Be light. Be warm. For instance, you cannot go to the park because you do not have time to take them into the park, but two days later, as planned, you will take them.
- Please be good at your words. Do so, if you say something. Otherwise, it would make you lie.
- Do not be accusative, because your child is being told about a case to learn the facts. If you fear, for example, that your son has got a lamp in your living room, do not hurry up and call out to him: "I think you have struck a lamp, better tell me what you are doing right now." This tells him just to hide the evidence because the reality makes him uncomfortable.
- Think about the victims and the way their mistakes and ties have been hurt as you admit to lying. Test the marriages, which are negative and frustrating.
- Praise your child for the honesty he has expressed, mainly if it is difficult to tell the goodness.

Help Him Finding Out His Strengths & Desires

It is difficult to be perfect if you are not sure about what you are doing. It is the same thing for our girls. If we want to be successful, we have to learn what our children enjoy in life. Learning what they are good at, their talent and passion intersect, which is the best path for finding achievement and happiness.

Parents ought to be attentive in recognizing their children's talents and innate ability. Then give them a chance to explore their skills and to turn them into a routine, if your son enjoys doing it. For instance, you might want to involve your kid in a footballing season and love shooting a target in your backyard at night if you see a proper alignment of your hand and eye with a goal. If he preserves his skills and enjoys sport, it will become a passion. To learn to buildability with passionate dedication is an essential talent to succeed in their lives. If you are never enthusiastic about something, it is hard to get motivated while working hard.

You will discover the ability to look closely and strive hard to find happiness. This helps one to establish positive work ethics in the long term. It would make them glade as men. You, as a mother, should help your child in think about issues and events that make them exciting about their young lives so that they can find opportunities to develop their talents to work for a cause.

Instruct Productive Practices of Growing

Individuals with insufficient care may have issues with their relationships and their jobs. I interviewed in a skewed suit, bad breath, and body fragrance, and the interviewer is told that the task is not sufficiently important to try, look, and smell good. It is the opportunity to show all boys are essential to dress nicely and efficiently. You are going to learn how to use iron and how to match clothes correctly. Boys will always determine what proper hygiene and cleaning activities mean from an early age. Mothers need to teach their children how to wash their hair every day, how to cut their nails, shower every day, brush their teeth, change their shoes, and sometimes shower or bathe.

Often boys neglect proper hygiene to taking care of their bodies over time. That is where parents will engage and set particular criteria for grooming. For example, if your son refuses to shower and you rule to shower every other day because it has been a week now, then you will lose your social privileges because of computers, for example, before they wash. You learn how to look after the bodies as you practice them. Healthy grooming activities should be a ritual that starts as soon as you can brush your teeth. We do not know if this stuff can be achieved by osmosis.

We ought to explain how to experience the best grooming and personal treatment. In some instances, all problems can be overcome and avoided, including smelly clothes, body order, and greasy hair. Reasonable people must understand their sons how to have cleanliness and healthy habits.

The motivation for Knowledge and Understanding

If you want a mechanic, a hairdresser, or a neurosurgeon, your son must be educated. Wisdom is power, you know. The day we decide to quit rising is the day we no longer have to know anything more, which is why, as a life-long endeavor, we must instill in our children that we never end up with knowledge and learning. Offer your son the pleasure and happiness of education and learning. Enable him to find out that the books are going to inspire him to do what he wants. Of course, he would like Lacrosse's sport.

He does not know anything about the competition, so he looked at the game and wanted to try it out and maybe join the team. He is expected to brace himself so he should hear about the sport. The support in sports is incredibly important; however, the rules and how to properly use the equipment and the techniques to make one a better athlete are always beneficial.

Before he goes on the field, he will watch a book at Lacrosse Library. He must be able to learn the sport to be successful at it. However, it is not essential to learn about schools and books alone. It is a life and mentoring commodity. There can just be a desire to do something good. By combining the acquired knowledge and experience, we will also be able to learn and improve.

How to Respect Others Tell Them?
Boys are also children, never an adequate source of misbehavior. The area is beginning to have positive behavior anticipation. Children, particularly elders and women, must be trained in honoring others. We should carry this belief into their enrolment, jobs, and adult life with them as they are at home taught to make women younger.

We prefer to respect boys as women are assumed to be equal to them. Will they have the same qualifications? Yet for different talents that do not make us weaker, so it just affects us. Encourage people as children to respect the qualities and ideals of women to benefit children and girls. You would also be a great wife, a great partner, and an attraction for the same sex in the future. This would undoubtedly be said and backed up with these ideas as it is learned that women are inferior to men or that they should be valued.

Our feelings and values are the driving force behind our actions. In our life, our acts are changed. The society has serious and omnivorous issues with domestic violence and sexual assault. Many offenders are men and women with much higher weight. Household shelters are an awareness-raising organization for domestic violence. We claim that 85% of domestic violence victims are women.

Children must be told that harassment is unacceptable, especially to women. You will also be told that 'no' is 'no.' She will quit if a guy or a child says nothing about physical progress. When students are educated and taken to heart to help young girls, harassment of women is stopped. Nevertheless, during the years of puberty and adolescence, it would have been a regular conversation to think about how women are treated. It should not be a particular debate. Good behavioral habits and relationships are also significant. When a man abuses his wife, children who watch the trends of violence listen and understand. Never say your sons hit a woman, but you run your mother in the health of rage. Your words would speak louder than you presume.

Let Them Do Daily Physical Activity
Elevating boys is not easy. I do so myself as I know how to treat or monitor my twins more frequently. I know that they require lots of space and physical exercise facilities because most children are physiological. To seek and minimize resources as a result of their excellent scholarly success is like hunger and to expect an abundance of a boy. Children require more physical training to succeed in education. The time of play during the break is not enough. The study showed that the physical education of a child is more critical than in recesses. It means that it is necessary to play outside and play games, before and after school, to get their frustration out. They had not been required to sit at the desks for lengthy stretches but would sit all day at the classes. The reaction is that they work after school and before school for a long

time because they have to sit on a bench. Children lack physical activity and are more likely to plan and learn every day than in a timeline. They may have issues such as lack of focus, reduced academic performance, difficult reading, depression, anxiety, and anger because they cannot use their physical abilities. Boy's physical activity should be allowed daily, a few hours a day.

Most parents are denied a free celebration for their children because they are children playing either on or off the ground. They build adults who struggle for self-protection. They develop in the process. On the other hand, other parents go through the period they have schoolwork with their children to ensure that their little ones are outstanding. Study indicates that students are viewed basically as a daily work for their parents when their teachers attend.

Most of us are not involved in a closer relationship with our parents, but they are often good. Yeah, closeness, friendship, caring, sometimes contact between parent and child.

If you want your kid to be confident at age 18, you have to stop cutting their meat anywhere. But where do you cut meat?

Why do you not look for the two ways as you go around the road? When do you allow them to speak to the foreigners? This omnipresent over-implication means that the children must become adults while still stunted, relying upon their parents to raise their lives not only gradually, but also with their perfect, light, and etheric visions. What is great is not necessarily the joy of planning others' courses. Morality falls away in the refurbishing of their education, the cruel essence of being a perpetual crucible; the harm is done by transforming passion into success. In reality, the hardest part of all is this hidden message we are sending children: 'I suppose you should not.

The best thing is the cryptic message we post; we support them so that they are not weak, but they are abused, and we do so much. You are not good enough in this life; this is the message. That is the truth.

Some artists know that we want to inspire children to draw up the kinds of talents and principles that they have built-in their earliest days. When using smartphones and engaging in social media, well before formal education, they encountered vigorous academics. The genuine issue is to make our kids advance. We minimize the essentials of schooling and enable children to become doers, the people who are prepared to deal with what will be an uncertain future, and plan to recognize, achieve, and protect their vision of achievement. You do not have to eliminate all traditional aspects of your life today, but we will ensure that children do not miss the simple moments.

The World Must Be Discover by Kids

Children have a lot to do, talk, and play by their hands with their parents. Children must be allowed to communicate with the world, even as a children's museum, where the discovery is accepted without any restrictions. The essential learning of unstructured sports reduces the amount of scheduled play and the time spent with the game.

Knowledge of Developments

Kids are the answers to simple problems. They check cause and effect hypotheses along with understanding the trial and error. These skills may be promoted by adults or quashed. Children deserve to be safe when subjected to unstructured activities. Drawing pictures, building blocks, clay modeling, and the opportunity for a child to work without guidance and input can assist children in discovering their artistic selves. Parents will support this process by providing clearly-developed incentives, encouraging and cultivating the joy of learning, and the desire to go over the wall.

Kids Nowadays Learn from Enthusiasm
Children will learn to push a bike without training wheels, to criticize a school teacher, to address what a peer needs to achieve, and to determine future steps towards success. Parents may encourage children to talk through challenges.

Kids Are Tracker of Prospect
Under the shade of the umbrella, children will not have to act that they cannot be reckless, however, rather than focusing on risk-taking, it encourages children to know how to manage the potential difficulty (and see from them) so that people realize the value of self-challenge. If a kid wants to scale a tree a little high, it could be "hand-off; still, eyes locked."

It is not all about competition. Make sure a child has a safe hand-hold even though the answer is not understood. Teach the kids, and it is well to play in kindergarten, even if they are a bit shy on stage. Commemorate involvement and stability rather than "big profits."

Children's Take Crappy Duty
Why should kids perform their job? Children will not only be willing to compete according to age but understand that you cannot expect anyone to perform all the dirty tasks. Help children engage in social activities and learn to be their partner alongside others and achieve what they need without being afraid and handle it alone. Let them

know that you do not matter to the universe, and those who tend to do their job are becoming successful citizens.

Social Abilities Are Deceptive
They tend to focus on predicting adult achievements by studying how to get along early in life with other youngsters. Instead of stumping and proactively screaming, children will learn how to cope with disagreements. Working together is a skill that is nurtured in childhood. Working encourages parents to do work together as a team to promote a project. Communication is vital; it can compensate for talking to children and developing their communication skills at all levels later on.

Children Should Support Other Children
Evidence suggests that, unless they are offered the chance, even girls are future aides. See if your child will catch it and drop it when you spill it. In exchange, you do need a thank you.

Some works suggest that treating a child as a "good mate" gives him a feeling of caring. Explain how we are both going to find opportunities to support the vulnerable and model empathy, along with concern. Computers and piano lessons were not overlooked. Make sure you allow your children ample room to improve all their abilities at home before they exit the nest.

How to Avoid Over-parenting?

A parent is one of the most versatile yet lucrative roles on the planet. Specific safety tasks can appear terrifying or daunting, so it can overwhelm you.

Overpaid children sometimes pick themselves or exist in hardship alone. You will avoid this by having your child develop trust, endurance, obstacles, and coping with your usage. You can do that. You should do that. That is what we all want. Why is the connection broken?

Learn about four steps to prevent overfriendliness and provide your children with the most exceptional opportunity to be happy, safe, and successful. We find that flight, helicoptering, and micro administrators are another concept which we do not know in the first two-part series. Parents do what they can. What they should do for their kids is considered over-parenting, when you try to fix or prevent your children's faults that are over-parenting.

We also gave two or three (more or less) theories, as most of us do: the college hunt, the apprehension of risky, and the self-harming actions.

The main fear is that children may commit irreparable errors and mistakes. Instead of calmly addressing the issue, it is named sad, creative, and futuristic. The children use the expression, "I do not think you can do it yourself, so I am going to do it," so adults do not defend themselves unnecessarily.

Furthermore, adolescents understand that another good argument to prevent over-parenting is the idea and perception to paralyze our children from relationships and jobs. You quit thinking about yourself slowly, and you avoid problem-solving. You remember you are not apologizing for yourself. You learn. Why take from the earth your dirty clothes? What happens if your parents seek to lower their grades or accuse a school problem? Another outcome is the damage that is prevented.

Have you have ever noticed that the response of your body is to do more, not less, especially with your children, when things are not perfect?

Somewhat of walking out, you will lift your voice because you worry. You run in with lots of thoughts if you battle with the rough, rather than staying silent or offering any suggestions. A quieter voice will more effectively draw attention, and your few recommendations will motivate you to devise more of your strategies. There is also an evident perception that our children require more time, more resources, more commitment, and more kindness in our community as they fight.

Stop Loss, Debate, and Exchange
This can refer to particular children and adult parents, but it is not every time true. It is also an excellent way to discourage our children from having all of these items. So, if we live out of affection in this manner, we are going to create the very opposite outcome. Instead of self-reliance, we implicitly promoted dependency. Children are being addicted. Eventually, they learn impotence instead of endurance.

Tolerance of Children
We often understand that it is essential to fulfilling the needs and expectations of others to

be a good parent, family, or partner. That is relevant, but just to a certain extent. If there is more to the reaction: was it better than less now, then?

There are multiple instances.

- Do something about yourself and less about your kids. Under this case, it is a more caring and diligent method for a mother to do less empathizing and meeting her needs and to put further focus on kids.
- Fewer worries for addressing the expectations of children and empowering them more to assume responsibility for themselves. Being careless about the feelings of children and more about helping them behave in the best possible way. For instance, I am not going to know much more, so you should get the missing homework books. You have to find out what is right for tomorrow to do something.
  You do not want to confess to your aunt that you are sorry, so I keep you accountable for doing the right thing.
- Think less about purchasing and grubbing away, and more about managing and ruling themselves. I realize that I do not like your work, but I want them to be finished before I expect you to finish them. You might be frustrated, but please do not find a way to pull others down because you are not happy. Please be near your kids in the manner they need you, but then, stay

away from them. With this, we also know how to understand the distance.

When teachers, attorneys, and relatives advise you that your children appear to require more from you, which is attention, endurance, time, kindness, stop thinking hard. Will they do that? Were you going to neglect them? If so, you can do more than you should, of course, and, in the likely event, they get more than enough of you.

It is much better if you slit your legs and make it difficult to reach them. Letting go will render you feel wobbly first. However, you can notice your heavy legs standing through practice and time.

Influence of parents and the power of connection with children

How do parents act the way they do while they are parenting children? Another theory is that they emulate the actions of their parents. Who has experienced how to be a mom through the process of parenting?

Another is that they behave in compliance with knowledge on effective parenting obtained by books, blogs, or informal and formal guidance. An additional significant determinant of their actions is their overall behaviors, as well as the fundamental values, emotions, and feelings that are triggered through parenting. In essence, they have a substantial effect on their behavior, mainly though their parents are depressed or oblivious of the influence. Researchers involved in the growth of children have examined parenting behaviors, cognitions, and related feelings (such as frustration or happiness) due to their effect on parenting behavior and the resultant effects of parenting activity on children's socio-emotional and cognitive progress.

Kid-rearing practices are cognitions that tend to lead a person to behave either positively or negatively towards an infant. Attitudes more commonly discussed represent the degree of warmth, approval, or coldness and disapproval that occurs in the parent-child partnership. As well as the level to which parents are permissive or stringent within the boundaries that they set for their children. Scientists have also analyzed more condition-specific thoughts or schemes that are channels by which parents perceive and respond to the incidents, particularly ambiguous ones. They involve cognitions such as assumptions with regard to leadership abilities, perceptions of what children are capable of or would be allowed to do, and explanations why children have acted in a particular manner.

The effect of attitudes on parenting practices has been a favorite topic of study, with studies showing that ties are typically modest. This is partially attributed to the reality that recorded behaviors do not often have a definite effect on parental behavior that is mostly aimed at particular circumstances. Parents may, for example, support or respect being pleasant and attentive to children, but have trouble in voicing such feelings while their child is misbehaving. As a consequence of this understanding, the study of parent cognitions has been expanded to involve more complex forms of thought. Analysis in parent behaviors, value structures, and action has taken place along with increasing child-rearing principles. Such shifts also demonstrated the bi-directional complexity of the relationships, with children influencing parents as well as parents impacting babies.

Consequently, an essential continuation of the study on perceptions and cognitions has to do with how the behavior of children influences the attitudes and emotions of parents. However, little research has been done in this field.

As a parent, how to gain (and lost) influence on children

Any parent who needs control, and while a parent is the most significant impact in the life of a child, it will broaden through the seasons. Many parents, in reality, I know they feel and lack control.

The impression is essential to be taken care of irrespective of the level of the parentage, as any parent is eventually moving from authority to power. We continue with almost complete control over the life of an adult, but when our children are eighteen and ready for the experience alone, we all have left is impact.

Five simple ways to lose power as a parent are accessible:

1. **This effects risk, but rarely execute them:**

The children will know that they will never believe anything you say.

2. **Shame and anger to your children**: They are going to try to move as far as possible from you.

3. **Try to be a good friend of your children:** The children deserve more guardians than any friend does.

4. **Behavior with your partner:** Your children would quickly lose respect.

5. **Be unpredictable:** You will lack faith in you if your children never realize where you are.

6. **Power will soon be forgotten**: However, how can you win? Whose ability would you cultivate? How can you develop a safe and lasting relationship?

Below are some ways to boost your effect on children:

1. **Do what you said:** Exactly what you thought you would do before you agreed that you would do something. It fosters confidence, trust, and even love.

2. **Implement limits:** you should not accept that by having your children with their obligations, boundaries, and expectations off the hook you are supporting. They are going to reward you for that one day.

3. **Treat with kindness to others:** Be kind to the people closest to you (it is reasonable, of course, to do the contrary).

4. **Do not overdo your kid:** Let recompenses. You should not praise your children with something, or just follow as they anticipate.
5. **Work on your character:** You would have a more substantial impact over their own lives as your children see you grow your faith and character.

If you learn all about this, you possibly exhibit some of the characteristics already mentioned, people over which you have an impact. You love and admire them because people are responsible, caring, and compassionate, who have a strong conscience and stand for everything.

Those who lack control over their lives become unreliable and socially unstable men. Although discipline is required to grow your character and stick to specific boundaries as a parent, it can allow you to exert and retain an impact on your children over time. Ultimately, all we have left for our children, in either case, is power.

CHAPTER 8: WHEN CAN PARENTS MOST INFLUENCE THEIR CHILD'S DEVELOPMENT?

Human and other studies have repeatedly clarified biological embedding mechanisms, wherein systemic and functional effects are integrated into the material and social environments under which production occurs. These effects become particularly marked when the design, structure, and control of the processes are developed in the fetal and early postnatal development. Parents have a significant influence on the actions of their children. Children are like seashells, all that a parent can create, so they absorb into their own lives what they see. Parents should give the best expectations for their children. Bad experiences can affect the growth of a child and contribute to negative behavior.

Impact of Social Skills

Social skills can be described as anything from the simple friendly "please" and "thank you" to interacting in front of the audience. Kids learn from their peers.

The Stressed-Out Inheritance

The parent's response to stress influences the way a child reacts to stress. If the parent responds adversely, the infant may always begin to respond negatively. In regards, negative responses to anxiety, such as screaming and shouting, can frighten a child.

Kids can learn to close themselves away as well as think that they are the cause of depression. When depression is dealt with respect, it allows children to know that their parents' affection for them never decreases, except though they are stressed out.

Maintain Positive Discipline

As described earlier, the way parents intervene to profoundly affects the actions of their children. When a parent wants to use physical discipline, such as spanking, the kid is not shown how to modify his actions. Children can often respond violently to physical restraint. As parents use alternate methods of discipline, such as time-outs, they tend to change the harmful conduct of the infant gently.

Frenzy War

If the dispute among the parents is rational and reasonable, the advantage of a child is to see how disputes are handled. Verbal and physical fighting is particularly difficult for girls. Kids will blame themselves on the claims of their parents and traumatize themselves in future years. Children may experience poor self-esteem and even physically interfere with other children. In their subsequent marriages, children frequently replicate this behavior.

Threatens Domestic Abuse

Children neglect the causes of a variety of anti-social and harmful behaviors. This is how victimized children tend to cope with and understand why they are victimized. Parents who neglect their children may make their children angry and abusive, have learning disabilities, and may even indulge in alcohol or drugs.

Parents that exploit have the opposite of a child's safe development. Instead, they are destroying a child's inner and outer world.

The Consequences of Poor Parenting on Kids

The effect of the parents on their children appears to be misunderstood. Two times more likely to be misbehaved is in children who are subjected to poor parenting. Inconsistent disciplinary methods, inadequate oversight, and physical discipline are weak parental skills, which, irrespective of ethnicity and socioeconomic status, may have a negative effect on children.

Anti-Social Comportment
Whenever a kid has antisocial behavior, they do not care about how their practices can hurt others. Severe forms of anti-social behavior can result in drug abuse, alcohol abuse, poor health, mental health, unemployment, and crimes for adults. Inconsistent and strict maternal treatment, including maternal substance misuse, mothers' addiction, including domestic violence, may contribute to parenting patterns that may help to this form of behavior. Adults with permissive, manipulative, pessimistic behaviors, and positive attitudes may have antisocial tendencies more likely to have offspring.

Deprived Flexibility
Flexibility implies the capacity of a person to overcome psychological, mental, behavioral, physical, and educational difficulties. Families with weak resistance have children who often have low flexibility.

In this respect, poor parenting is the fact that the children do not cover up the negative consequences of disaster and does not encourage a child to adapt and to respond in times of need. If a child has low tolerance, this may be because a parent is inflexible, cannot deal with transitions well, or cannot cope in a balanced way with negative feelings.

Depression
Hard and pessimistic parenting contributes to infant distress symptoms. Their total care level, maternal stress, physical punishments, inadequate health manifestations of depressive feelings, and lack of social stimulation are all the causes that may contribute to childhood stress.

Violence
Weak parenthood led to sexual abuse through infancy. The mothers studied how their children were treated roughly, showed their children negative feelings, and worsened conflicts. The researchers found that the children who were examined exhibited a higher degree of rage, leading mothers to become more aggressive. The bond between mother and father was not investigated. How may this have affected the feelings or actions of the mother?

Types of Parenting Style
Family-related leadership patterns differ and can change in one household every day. Each parent often makes stringent or more lenient choices for their children. The reason one parent slides into one of the three common forms of parenting is in the majority of situations. There are conservative, permissive, and egalitarian types of childhood.

Commanding

The parents of authority are robust, affectionate, and loving. We set boundaries and encourage their kids to stick with them. No unnecessarily stringent or extremely lenient parents strike a reasonable balance between unrealistic and unreasonable expectations.

These parents require their children to make age-specific decisions and empower them to be more responsible as they mature. They answer well to your child's needs but do not fulfill all wishes. They give their kids explanations for such rules and instructions and encourage reasonable consequences to be done as far as possible even where no real harm is caused to the infant. Children of authoritarian parents also show a strong sense of social competence, freedom, and obligation as younger adults grow up.

Dictatorial

Strict, unbending, and inflexible parents are totalitarian. They can try and not let the child make choices to influence every part of the life of their child. Authoritarian parents demand unquestioned compliance. To their children, parents may apply strict forms of punishment and be indifferent to the needs of their children. Sometimes they do not clarify the reasoning behind the rules they set because, when a rule is broken, they enforce their repercussions. Adult children of authoritarian parents will have trouble voicing themselves without a clear guide.

Accommodating

Restrictive parents are self-satisfied and do not want to control the developing nature of their adults. We will also not create laws and have little to do with them. They might drive the child to escape even reasonable or rational outcomes to save the child from potential harm, unhappiness, or hurt. Permitted parents are generally kind and affectionate but can be frustrated if the behavior of a child is distrustful or unforgivable. Notwithstanding this resentment, parents who have trained themselves sometimes do not alter the functioning of the child so as long as it is not physically harmed. Allowable parenting may result in adolescents and young adults becoming self-centered or self-regarding.

CHAPTER 9: COMPLICATIONS IN OVERPROTECTION IN CHILDREN

In the early days of their childhood, as children develop from complete withdrawal to greater freedom in their adolescence, they tend to experience the need for their own identity. Parents may feel excessively defending their children and would like to monitor their entire lives in fear of dangers such as narcotics, alcohol, school abuse, teenage pregnancies, and pedophiles. Parents ought to learn the difference between being active and being overprotective of their children's lives.

Loose Self-Confidence
Overly possessive parents give a message that their offspring cannot meet the pressures of life alone. Such children can result in a lack of self-confidence. They may believe like they cannot thrive in life without the leadership by their parents because their parents do not trust them in the ability to make mistakes and to solve issues on their own.

Power Illusion
Parents often may assume that they are able to safeguard their children by overprotecting them. This will result in an illusion of power over their kids who may revolt as this illusion gets older and broken.

Risk Talking
When children reach puberty, they often spend more time beyond their parents' reach. This independence could offer children, and overprotective parents, more risk-taking actions.

Teens may be more vulnerable to involvement in alcohol consumption or substance misuse in sexual practices. Young kids also challenge their parents' expectations as confident children have not developed a sense of obligation. The duty has also been carried on by over-protective parents. Have a discussion with the young adult about risk-taking and how the consequences can be detrimental to issues like drugs or alcohol.

Self-Possession

The lack of self-esteem growth in a child may result in overprotection by parents. This is because, without parental intervention, the infant is not able to face obstacles. A part of infant self-esteem is a product of self-conscious struggles, so overprotective parenting should be ignored.

What are the key features of a good parent?

A good parent allows children to develop values, including integrity, patience, self-management, self-reliance, co-operation, happiness, and compassion, which motivates them. A healthy parent also helps and protects from psychiatric issues, including stress, anxiety, and anti-social behavior, which raises the risk of substance addiction.

Loving and Caring

To raise healthy children is most important, and it must be followed by caring and affectionate behavior while offering parental guidance. Caring parents do not tend to criticize and blame their children for love, support, and nurturing.

They develop self-esteem rather than challenging it through the use of positive reinforcement. They immediately deliver enthusiastic praises anytime, so their child achieves an achievement. A caring parent might say that I am so proud that you made the basketball team.

Competent Conversationalists

Parents who are professional communicators are sincerely involved and available to them in all aspects of their child's life. To be a successful communicator, allow your child to voice his / her thoughts and then listen to them. Having an active reader reflects his respect and admiration for his opinions and views.

Capability for Stress Management

The ability to withstand tension and anger, which leads to well-fit babies, is another essential trait of a successful parent. Often children cope with pressure by observing how their parents treat feelings under challenging circumstances. If parents cannot cope with stress, it also leads to anxiety and less support for their children. Your child will follow your example and know how to deal with tension themselves.

Autonomy Cooperative

Rebellion is also a necessary part of the child's sovereignty initiative. Parents who respect the growing freedom of their child tend to cultivate it instead of seeking to cool it. They ask for input from their kids instead of dictating laws and making a set of rules for a typical activity. Kids allowed to engage in decision-making are encouraged to do so. When your kid declined to play a video game and went to bed, you would be able to consent to a compromise by suggesting that you should play an additional 15 minutes, but then you are dormant.

Productive Role Model

A positive role model is more important than specific corrective steps or instructions in raising the children. Kids learn through learning and also mimic their parents' behavior. They feel less secure when they see their parents fighting and losing control. They could try, like their parents, to settle problems through fights and arguments. However, parents are good role models, who are capable of resolving disagreements and issues through quiet conversations without heated debates. Be the characteristics you want your child to grow like:

- Patience
- Tolerance
- Love
- Respect
- Kindness
- Compassion
- Honesty

Things we should do to empower outstanding individuals, who understand and learn how to use their unique qualities:

01. Enclose with pure love anything you do
02. Assume that every child is different and unique
03. Find challenges as winning
04. Always use positive language
05. Courage to accept changes
06. Build interests in your child
07. Develop capability
08. Properly communicate with kids
09. Explore opportunities to give them back
10. Form a community
11. Give time to watch sports
12. Share valuable things on social media

13.   Magnify your prospect
14.   Play games with your children
15.   Have a recreation trip

Enclose with Pure Love Anything You Do
With crazy, unshakable love, strengthen your bond with your kids. Be sure they understand you will like them irrespective of what they do, what they do or who they are. Say it, prove it, and live the joy of unconditional love. That does not mean they all care. Keep them following their goals. This is an essential part of life. They need restrictions, and they like them. Kids like boundaries of devotion. In the final lesson, we all have to know his unconditional love, which encompasses not only others but also us.

Assume That Every Child Is Different and Unique
Your child as lovely as any other kid in the country. See and applaud every child's abilities. Avoid comparing children with children you meet or their relatives. Let any child be himself. Let your child grow and emotionally develop every day. You have enough time to know. You would not always be the stubborn, strong-willed boy. They will mature into a young person who is incredibly passionate and loving. Offer them freedom and give them space. You have to be bold to become who you are.

Find Challenges as Winning

From the day we start today, we finish; life will bring challenges. Train the kids to see problems as a reality and conquer together. What will we do to fix this? Talk about problems. What do we need? What works? What else can we do? So, if your child's struggle is yours, ask him questions, so give him his answers. Life is a fact to be learned, not a problem, to be solved.

Always Use Positive Language

Research indicates the power of the mind in creating positive behavior and shaping it. If we believe we can grow up an odd child, we shall. Perhaps our children would even doubt their success if we doubt our leadership any move on the way.

Often people become what they think they are. If I continue to suggest that I cannot do a sure thing, I might end up being completely unable to do it. On the opposite, if I think I can, I will develop the confidence to do so even though I cannot look at first.

Courage to Accept Changes

Each day, every milestone of development marks a change. Believe that it is fun to adjust and get ready for the next. It is part of the ride every day. Parenthood or childhood is never over. You enjoy the stage, instead of skipping ancient times or the long wait for the next step. Live and enjoy these moments timely. Your children are not going to be at that age again. They would not have the same parent still, either. You also rise and develop. Give the best you have got today to them. It was over yesterday, and it would not be there tomorrow. Realize deeply that you all have the current time.

Build Interests in Your Child
Play outdoor games, listen to music, and explore future interests. Expose your children as far as possible to as many places and people. Travel whether from a distant location you are willing, or have a pen pal. Show them what their position will be in the world. What is yours? Tell them what you are doing or what you dream one day of doing. Show them how your inspiration can be found. The day when you are born and the day when you figure out why are the two most important days of your life.

Develop Capability
Let them fight. Enable them to do their tasks after working hard. Children who believe that something like cooking is dangerous or difficult will lose a lifetime or even years to master this ability. It is not what you are doing for your kids, but what you have taught them to do will make them happy.

Properly Communicate with Kids

We have to tell our kids how to brush their teeth or fold a shirt; coordination is required. Continue to talk to them. In the meanwhile, listen to them as well. Tell yourself questions and talk politely, most notably. See reasons made simple, or what is your type of communication? When you chat, you just repeat what you know, but you will learn something new when you listen.

Explore Opportunities to Give Them Back

Working for others is kindness, love, and compassion for others. Allow children the opportunity to give them back. Perhaps this is in your own home, in education, in your city or the world in general. Enable them to plan or take part in a drive at school. Let them play if there is a fun race. As a family, donate things you no longer need or send to the local shelter. Connecting children with people and their families help them to cultivate compassion. What do you do for others is life's most pressing question?

Form a Community

Seek your people and build a home with them. Build family bonds and keep the ups and downs of those bonds close to each other. See your family, neighbors, and your children's peers with their abilities and useful points. Take a look at the powers, and they can draw on them too. Your whole group is sturdy and robust. Give more than you get. Say your friend's children to be babysitting indeed. Say yes to family holidays.

Say yourself yes for dinner or a trip. They trust them more as the qualities of the kids are used by many. When the kids see conditions in others, they grow talents without understanding them. Using and being supported by your family, you have to raise a child in a village. Individual children are raised in exemplary families. Discover and enjoy a place in your culture. You will be more relaxed and optimistic, and your kids' tolerance would improve. You have grown comfortability with the fact that you can live with whatever life throws.

Give Time to Watch Sports

It will not only be an enjoyable way to interact with a favorite team and athlete, but also it would offer a perfect chance to point out the qualities of a character from teamwork to determination. After cheering on a big hit or basketball, point out how vital the linebackers or transfers were for achieving the result while they did not get the spotlight, without a great job of supporting players, the squad would not be successful.

Share Valuable Things on Social Media

Social media is full of character teachings from Facebook to YouTube. Share it with your child and remark about how bold it was for the boy to share his story or artistic speech when you see a message, polo, or video of something particularly stunning or touchy. Address the dangers inherent in putting yourself forward and the value of taking (reasonable) chances, even though you may be attacked.

Magnify Your Prospect
Watching documentary films featuring very different individuals will cause empathy, sympathy, and modesty. Choose something out of the ordinary at a family movie night. A movie about someone of another race or faith, or a less privileged society and a subculture of different ideals or views from yours, and encourage conversation afterward.

Play Games with Your Children
Playing games as a group provides the ability to work together, solve challenges, connect and persevere, while still enjoying the fun. Then select multiplayer games in which you have to work with players to win. Implement useful and polite contact in the game. You will notice their contributions and their progress if kids actively seek to accomplish a game goal.

Take a Recreation
Most households are daunting as different mobile apps alert us about social media and text messages. By avoiding the temptation to respond automatically, we will help our children to learn about themselves. You will get a text message warning, next time around, so you know there is no rush. Consequently, you will say softly, "I do not have to test right now."

CHAPTER 11: HOW TO IMPROVE CONNECTIONS BETWEEN PARENTS AND CHILDREN?

Enhancing relationships between parents and children involves commitment and energy. Parenting is a challenging job, but parents can stay linked to them in all the periods of life by keeping a close relationship and open contact with their children.

Furthermore, as children who feel more connected with their parents are more likely to listen, support, and follow instructions, a good parent-child relationship also makes parenting even easier. Children who feel connected are often prepared to speak to their parents about issues with peers and educators. Ten easy tips families can use to strengthen connections between children and parents are:

- **Show your love and affection**

- **Play in spare time**
- **Call your loving kid with a unique name**
- **Maintain bedtime rituals**
- **Teach your children religion and spirituality**
- **Teach your children to help you**
- **Arrange family meals**
- **Arrange special events**
- **Children's choice of respect**
- **Give your life a priority.**

Show Your Love and Affection

Tell kids every day, regardless of age; you love them. Particularly in days of difficulty or frustration, parents will ensure that children know you love them unconditionally when you do not like their actions. Conflicts make parents express their love for their children is the most critical moment. A basic "I love you" works best to establish relationships.

Play in Spare Time

The trick is to get down and to play with your family. No matter what you do, just enjoy yourself and devote yourself to paying unparalleled attention. Let your children look at your dumb face. Older children enjoy cards, chess, and computer games, while younger children enjoy playing with their parents.

Call Your Loving Kid with a Special Name
Develop a name that is good for your kid or a hidden code word you will use together. Use the title to strengthen your love. The codeword should be used to withdraw a child from an uncomfortable situation without giving the child an unnecessary humiliation, such as a sleep-over that does not work well.

Maintain Bedtime Rituals
Lifelong habits are generated by reading books or sharing children's stories. Bedtime is a break. It helps children feel better by having a routine. Bedtime may also be the only time parents interact with their children, so try to keep quiet for fun. As soon as children begin to read, you can read them a page, a section, or a short book. While most young adults also love the practice of making a particular adult say goodnight.

Teach Your Children Religion and Spirituality
Teach the confidence and conviction to your kids. Tell them what and why you think. Give your child time to inquire and respond frankly to the questions.

Teach Your Children to Help You
Parents often unwittingly miss out chances for closeness by not having their child to support them with different activities and chores. Unloading shopping when going to the store is an excellent example of something that children of

most ages can and should help. If they support, children feel good. Through opinion, children can also help. Ask a kid who looked better in her dress lets her know that you value her thoughts. Be able to embrace and abide by the preferences of the child if you ask.

Arrange Family Meals
It is genuinely significant. Food sets the tone for dialogue and communication together. Switch off the television and do not run for a meal. Speak and enjoy each other when schedules allow. This will become a moment of consistency that young and old alike recall.

Arrange Special Events
Many parents have regular evenings with their babies or stand dates to build this one-on-one chance. It is essential to enjoy every child uniquely, whether it is a stroll through the school or a special trip to a park or even a film night with both of you. While for parents of many children, this is more than a struggle, it is attainable.

Children's Choice of Respect
At an early age, children achieve maturity, and parents will help to encourage these decision-making capabilities through encouragement and even look the other way. After all, it is fine for a child to go to kindergarten with a streaked green shirt and pink shorts.

CONCLUSION

Your kids will know that in their life, you think that they are a priority. Children can notice excessive stress when they feel that they do not pay attention to them. Parenthood sometimes does not ponder about the little things, and your children enjoy. They grow up so quickly and become amazing every day. Take advantage together of your precious time.

When you are underage, this is extremely important. Parents who educated their children when they were young are the most successful parents. It is just the best way to learn. We were always there; you also tell your children to be like a self-pilot. If you do so, your child will be more interested in education. Ask them to read bits of books. Tell them the story. Tell them to modify the chapters for you if they are too impressionable. "What are you going to do if you were the baby boy?" she asks. "Even in books that you read 216 times together, the child can come up with a new answer every character will create. This book will help the parents to grow their kids. Parents will learn many things from this book and they will be happy after following each and everything.

COPYRIGHTS

This book:

"**HOW TO RAISE AN ADULT:** Prepare Your Kid for Success! How to Raise a Boy! Break Free of the Overparenting Trap, Increase Your Influence with the Power of Connection to Build Good Men"

Written by James Goodchild.

the written permission of the publisher and all liberties authorized.

The information provided here is correct and reliable, as any lack of attention or other means resulting from the misuse or use of the procedures or instructions contained therein is the total and absolute obligation of the user addressed.

The author is not obliged, directly or indirectly, to assume civil liability for any restoration, damage, or loss resulting from the data collected here. The respective authors retain all copyrights not kept by the publisher.

The information contained herein is solely and universally available for information purposes. The data is presented without a warranty or promise of any kind.

The trademarks used are without approval, and the patent is issued without the trademark owner's permission or protection.

The logos and labels in this book are the property of the owners themselves and are not associated with this text.

BRAIN TRAINING & MEMORY IMPROVEMENT

Accelerated Learning to Discover Your Unlimited Memory Potential, Train Your Brain, improve your Learning-Capabilities and Declutter Your Mind to Boost Your IQ!

BY

James Goodchild

TABLE OF CONTENTS

COPYRIGHTS

the written permission of the publisher and all liberties authorized.

The information provided here is correct and reliable, as any lack of attention or other means resulting from the misuse or use of the procedures or instructions contained therein is the total and absolute obligation of the user addressed.

The author is not obliged, directly or indirectly, to assume civil liability for any restoration, damage, or loss resulting from the data collected here. The respective authors retain all copyrights not kept by the publisher.

The information contained herein is solely and universally available for information purposes. The data is presented without a warranty or promise of any kind.

The trademarks used are without approval, and the patent is issued without the trademark owner's permission or protection.

The logos and labels in this book are the property of the owners themselves and are not associated with this text.

CHAPTER 1: INTRODUCTION TO MEMORY & MEMORY TRAINING

WHAT DOES MEMORY MEAN?

Memory is a crucial element of your intelligence. Everything you learn in life is organized and stored in some way. The efficiency in accessing this information defines the memory error. Scientists spend a lot of time looking for locations in the Brain where memories are stored and identifying the hippocampus and cerebral cortex as possible locations. Oppose to what we all think, and modern studies suggest that memory cannot be confined to a single part of the Brain. It is a mistake to think of storage as a storage device that fills everything. We have learned so far and looked into when we want to get information. Memories are activities and experiences, not places. When I remember something, I build it out of the details that I think it is most beneficial. Your Brain is explainable and can select, and the mechanisms that distribute throughout the Brain. Two people who have experienced the same event can get a completely different report. So, think about what the event means to you, not the exact details.

CAN YOU INCREASE YOUR MEMORY?

Absolutely! You can train, improve, and promote your memory. The information in your memory is affected by the meaning you give it. For example, remember that these are personal experiences and emotions. You can improve your memory skills by providing the information you need for more critical meanings and associations. Memories work by making something unforgettable, storing this personal information, and call it up at any time.

MEMORY CONCEPT

The things we have heard about it is our memory decreases with age. It is wrong, and if the Brain stimulates regularly, it can improve with age. People in the 80s and 90s can have the same memory as people in the six months. Brain cells do not die as we get older. Psychologist Tony

Busan reminds us that the essential memories do not necessarily belong to young people but to those who continue to improve their cognitive skills throughout their lives. Older people who are mentally stressed, learn new skills, and continue training may be mentally healthier than younger adults. Brain training offers good cognitive training. Here is a way to train your Brain and strengthen your memory. Come back to learn killer techniques.

HOW DOES MEMORY WORK?

Before we present the tips, let's look at the three types of storage that you need to receive and track.

SENSORY MEMORY

It receives information from senses such as seeing and hearing, processes it by holding it down for 1-2 seconds, and decides what you want to do. What you ignore quickly disappears and cannot do so often that the sound melts. Think about how you would see a sentence or echo from someone you know if you are not careful.

SHORT-TERM MEMORY

If you pay attention to something, the details transferred to the short-term memory can only save up to 7 data at a time. For example, you can only save your internet bank account number or your PIN code in this memory if you have to enter the key. As soon as short-term memory is "filled," no new neuronal mechanisms (meaning and associations) are created, and later information (i.e., data for removing old information) becomes available. Some scientists believe that evolution shaped this memory to have a limited capacity. Can you imagine keeping all the visual information you get in one day? What if you remember all the strangers you've passed and all the signs you've read? Well, your Brain will eventually experience data overload. The advantage of limited memory is that you can set priorities to focus on the task at hand.

LONG-TERM MEMORY

What does information transfer into long-term memory? All information can insert into this memory through the process of the rehearsal and the meaningful assignment. The processed data can be accessed weeks, months, or even years later. To do this effectively, you need to create as many links as possible to increase the number of starting points to save space, coordinate, review, and analyze information to make connections. Associations are mainly dependent on visual memory. It is an effective way to get a list of different items. One of the things we know about memory is that it is remembered rather than associated with personal experiences and emotions. If you are not sure, think about your birthday. What do you remember for 10, 15, 18, or 21 days? Probably 18 or 21 days because of its importance.

Everyone wants their brains to work optimally. It doesn't matter if you wish to keep up with your child or be at the top of the workplace. What is exciting is that science is now providing evidence of what works and what doesn't. So, training your Brain doesn't have to be an attempt to try one thing, determine that it doesn't work, and try something else. People who use the Brain more efficiently tend to have better jobs, better relationships, and a happy and more fulfilling life. And it's exciting. You can change your mind and thus your situation. You may have said that you were in your Brain a long time ago, but scientific research has shown that it is not! The plasticity of the Brain, the incredible ability of the Brain to adapt and change, is an exciting and growing field. And it's great that you can change your mind to make it work more effectively. Brain training doesn't have to involve a radical overhaul of your life. Here are some simple tips. Take a small blueberry on the way to the door. Play brain games on the move. Spend a few minutes every day. Find the best exercise to rejuvenate your Brain and enjoy the benefits of green tea. And discover the power of sleep in your heart.

NO MOTIVATION

Friendship not only increases motivation but also improves brain function! Just 10 minutes of social networking gives your Brain the same benefits as a crossword puzzle.

BRAIN TRAINING

I've heard of the left and right Brain. A heart is consisting of left and right hemispheres with different left and suitable functions. However, it is not entirely true that some people are "left brain" and others "right-brain." For example, language skills are in the left hemisphere, and everyone is using this part of the Brain! You do not have to hide behind the excuse that you are a right-brain to make your name unforgettable. Both halves of the Brain can achieve optimal values. There are key players in the world of brain training. Let's talk about how you can get attention. Most notably, different parts of the Brain do not work in isolation. They come together like a team. The training part of the Brain benefits the rest. You all must work together.

MEMORY TYPES

Long history Long-term memory consists of different types of memory.

AUTOBIOGRAPHICAL MEMORY

For example, childhood memories and meaningful events refer to as autobiographical memories. These types of memory are extreme, and their loss is an excellent early indicator of dementia and Alzheimer's. You can do a lot to keep these memories fresh.

MEANINGFUL MEMORY

Knowing the facts and random information called semantic memory can be handy when converting a new pointer from short-term to long-term memory.

PROCEDURAL MEMORY

Procedural memory is a mechanical skill that you do not even have to think. Driving or writing a name. You can find ways to automate new things to make your Brain work more efficiently. Short stories Short-term memory use to store linguistic, visual, and spatial information. If you do not "move" to a place in long-term memory, people usually do not remember anything in short-term memory for a very long time. The following are the ways to use short-term memory.

VERBAL

Do you remember what you said during the conversation? Do you remember how you stood on the stairs and why you went there? These are common phenomena and are not a sign of severe memory loss. However, if you want to keep your head shape, you can find ways to improve your language skills. Regardless of whether you want to keep an eye on your user list or age your memory, brain support can help you overcome the signs of Alzheimer's disease.

VISUALLY

Why are some people used to remembering their names but having difficulty remembering their names? An example of visual memory at work. Improve your Brain by using tricks to recognize your face and other types of visual information.

SPATIALLY

Are you always having trouble learning direction? Spatial memory is the key to achieving the right goal, not the wrong region. One of the tricks is a bird's eye view when you are in a new location. An active lifestyle leads to more efficient brain people, who react better, remember information, and can watch out for stress. What you eat, what exercises you do, how much sleep you get, and how much caffeine you drink, everything affects your Brain. It is essential to understand how daily decisions in these areas affect how the Brain works. So, before you drink another sandwich or wine, you should find one that suits your heart. Here is an overview of the tips and strategies you will find in this book.

EAT FOR YOUR BRAIN

Chocolate: It makes your Brain healthy. The Juice helps your memory. Steaks benefit your attention. Eating the right brain food doesn't mean eating salads or non-flavored foods. On the contrary, lots of delicious and beautiful foods filled with the proper nutrients for your Brain.

GET HELP FROM STIMULANTS

Caffeine, alcohol, drugs - these are all double-edged swords. In some cases, stimulants can help your Brain work better. However, many of these stimulants are expensive. Not all stimuli are the same. And you can do harm instead of your heart.

The Brain only weighs 3 pounds, but the whole body is still smooth. With 100 billion cells, your mind is like the CEO of a huge company. If you are wondering whether such small things have a great responsibility, you have come to the right place. This chapter contains some necessary information about how your Brain works. This understanding provides the basis for knowing how best to train your Brain.

DISCOVER THE FUNCTION OF THE BRAIN

Understanding the Brain has come a long way since the concept of four-touch humor (black bile, yellow bile, sputum, blood). According to the ancient Greeks and Romans, an imbalance in one of these moods causes illness and affects both mental and physical health. This general view persisted until the advent of modern medical research in the 19th century. Scientists are studying how the Brain works and making exciting discoveries every day. According to our current understanding, the Brain comprises of four parts.

BRAIN PARTS

FRONTAL LOBE

As the name suggests, the frontal lobe is in the front of the Brain and takes up most of the heart. One of the main functions of the frontal lobe is to plan and organize incoming information. When planning a party, drawing up a guest list, and managing the catering, the frontal lobe is crucial for carrying out all of these activities. The frontal lobe also helps regulate behavior and emotions. The Frontal lobe is associates with a chemical called dopamine. Dopamine is known as an area of brain pleasure because it is associated with reward and enjoyment. The frontal lobe does not appear until the age of 20. It can explain why it is difficult for a child to convince them not to experience a tantrum or why it is difficult for young people to consider the long-term consequences of their decision. In each of these scenarios, use the frontal lobe to plan the behavior, review the results, and change the action as needed.

PARIETAL LOBE

It is essential for the integration of information from various sources such as sensory and visual communication. The parietal lobe is divided into right and left hemispheres.

TEMPORAL LOBE

The temporal lobe is the home of language processing. The realm of humor lies in this part of the Brain. Part of the temporal lobe is responsible for visual information and object recognition. The temporal lobe is also home to another important player, the hippocampus.

OCCIPITAL LOBE

The occipital lobe is the smallest of the four lobes and lies in the back of the Brain. The visual cortex is responsible for visual processing information, motion detection, and color difference detection. This book doesn't touch that part of the mind very much. Elements of the mind are isolated and do not work. They work together as members of an orchestra. However, not all parts work together. In some cases, one element's performance may decrease while another element's performance may improve. This example shows the attention Deficit Hyperactivity Disorder.

BOTH SIDES OF THE BRAIN

The Brain composed of the left and right hemispheres connected by a "bridge" called the corpus callosum. But do you know that both sides of the Brain have different functions?

SAY HELLO ON THE LEFT SIDE OF THE BRAIN

Language is the most common characteristic of the left hemisphere. Grammar, vocabulary, and reading all relate to the left hemisphere. The left hemisphere is associated with language skills. Brain imaging studies show that general readers use the left occipital, temporal region, known as the word-formation region, to pronounce words as they read. Does the dyslexic Brain show the same pattern? A recent study looked at a 20-year-old group diagnosed with dyslexia in kindergarten. Brain imaging studies show little activation of the left temple area. Instead, 20-year-olds had higher activation of the right temple area. Some psychologists recommend people with dyslexia to bypass the left-brain mental pathways associated with phonological awareness skills and instead support reading in a more visually.

DO YOU KNOW THE RIGHT SIDE?

The right hemisphere controls the movement of the left side of the body. Responsible for spatial skills, facial recognition, and other visual processing. The right hemisphere also has thinking ability. Damaging this area can make inference more difficult, cause attention problems, and reduce the memory of graphical images. The researchers used the split-brain experiment to understand better how the right and left hemispheres work together. The brain part corpus callosum (the bridge between the two hemispheres) surgery recommendation is offered by Doctors to treat epilepsy. It prevents the information from crossing between the two hemispheres. The general experimental mechanism is as follows. The image is processed by the speech-sensitive left hemisphere so that the patient can easily recognize the image and call it a dog. However, if the image flashes on the left side of the computer (processed by the right hemisphere), the patient says that he cannot see anything! If the corpus callosum for linking information between the two hemispheres is not intact, the Right Brain cannot say what the left hemisphere sees, and thus a person translates what they see into language.

DOES YOUR BRAIN SHRINK WITH AGE?

The answer is yes! Like you think. If you grow 2% every ten years, brain training can make a difference. This contraction begins early in adulthood but only becomes noticeable at the age of 60. Higher brain contraction leads to dementia. So, some brain contraction is normal, but too much is a clear sign of problems like Alzheimer's and dementia.

TIPS TO AVOID

Keep the following tips in mind to avoid or at least delay principal brain contractions.

GIVE ALCOHOL

Studies have confirmed that alcohol is not suitable for your Brain. In addition to all the harmful effects, the heart will be smaller. Even light drinkers (and "light" means 1 to 7 alcoholic drinks a week) are affected by these alcohols in the Brain. Studies in humans in the 1960s have shown that even drinkers have less brain mass than those who do not. With more than 14 drinkers a week, heavy drinkers were the most affected by brain mass. Be especially careful with women. The female brain volume is more affected by alcohol than the male one. In other words, the effects of light drinking can be more pronounced in women than in men. Why does alcohol affect brain volume? Alcohol empties your tissues, and if this happens all the time, your most sensitive tissue and your Brain will slow down.

RELAX

Stress can also affect the Brain. It is especially true for repetitive stress, such as illness and work difficulties. The prefrontal cortex, which is associated with decision-making and attention, and the hippocampus, which is related to long-term memory, are most affected by stress. Stress makes it difficult for people to concentrate on the task at hand or to absorb new information. When people are under pressure, they lose the ability to be mentally flexible. So, when you face an immediate problem, it is difficult to solve it in a new and creative way.

The brain contraction was normal. However, this contraction does not have to affect the work of the Brain. Research shows that people in the 1960s and 1990s could "mitigate" the effects of brain contraction. Keep your mind active by learning new things. People who spend time discovering and learning something they do not know strengthen their Brain's protection from dementia and memory loss. By continuing your intellectual activity, you train your Brain mentally to keep it healthy in old age.

TIPS FOR IMPROVING BRAIN FUNCTION IN CHILDREN

TURN OFF COMPUTER GAMES

Some schools use certain computer games for this purpose. The game may be fun, but do you have any clues to improve learning? One study compared the benefits of certain computer games to playing Scrabble in elementary school. In your opinion, which group was the best memory test? It wasn't a computer game group; it was a group that played scrabble and word puzzles. So, if you want to power your kids up, the best thing to do is turn off your computer and buy Scrabble games instead.

THEY ARE NOT JUST MEMORY NUMBERS

Does remembering phone numbers improve your Brain? Some programmed brain training uses this approach. Students are trained for several weeks to learn random sequences daily or to place associations. Unfortunately, some students can achieve a higher working memory after training, but they do not improve immediately after exercise. Why? For the simple reason that these brain training programmers train to test - if the child remembers the number for weeks, the number test is of course better. These improvements are called exercise effects.

TRY IT IN THE JUNGLE

In my study, I wanted to confirm the metastatic effect of brain training. Does your child's brain training improve your learning outcomes? I saw a programmer named Jungle Memory, who trains working memory along with important learning activities like reading and math. I took a group of challenging students and randomly assigned them to one of two groups. Half of the students received brain training with jungle memory (training group), and the remaining students received targeted learning support at school (control group). Before starting the exercise, the students measured IQ, working memory, and learning outcomes. At the start of the research, both groups performed similar results on all of these cognitive tests. The fact is important. It means that the improvement that a child receives after training is the result of the activity and not the child that starts on another level. After training, the results were dramatic. The control group had no different results. In contrast, training groups using jungle memory significantly improved IQ, working memory, and, above all, learning outcomes.

HOW MUCH DO YOU LEARN FROM WATCHING?

According to a survey, about 76% of learning is visual. Take your baby, for example. They are curious and discover behavioral traits by watching what the people around them do. It processes and interprets facial expressions and body gestures. The baby can see briefly whether the mother is happy or angry. It doesn't always change. Imagine the two of them going out on their first date. How much attention do they have in conversation, and how much attention do they have when reading each other's body language? It is natural to get a lot of information from visual material since about 40% of the Brain takes on the function of displaying and processing graphic material. As a rough estimate, most people know the names of around 10,000 objects and cognize by their shape.

VISUAL

Your vision is the key to interacting with the world around you. The estimation shows that most children promise to remember the names of a fifth of the objects they know in their lives when they are six years old. Studies have shown that visual stimuli are most useful for brain development and more advanced types of learning, both during growth and in adulthood. People have different options for collecting information from more abstract graphic types such as spreadsheets, diagrams, the Internet, maps, and illustrations. By interpreting information from such sources, you can find meaning, reorganize, and group similar things, and compare and analyze different information. Your learning is arguably the most useful and widely used in education.

GET THE STEPS

The great thing about the visual part of the Brain is that when you look at it in a certain way, it tries to develop your memory. For example, when someone looks at someone else's performance to learn a dance sequence, the Brain attempts to collect, process, and remember visual information. You can then use memory to practice and develop your skills. Inspire your vision to learn new things.

VISUAL INSTRUCTIONS

The puzzles and exercises throughout the book contain essential visual elements. This principle shows that brain training programs enable specific interactions between words and images. This synergistic effect allows optimal training of the cognitive muscles. Some sources say that people who communicate with visual presentation tools are 43% more successful than those who do not.

SEEING MEANS BELIEVING

Of course, it is a maple leaf with the Canadian flag as a motif. By learning to respond in any situation, you can understand feelings that are difficult to describe in words. It gives your insight into your own deeper motives and can educate you about personal fears and frailty that you may not have noticed before. To access these emotions, create or search for a fictional story or fable. However, there are some similarities to the actual situation we are facing. Ideally, you can read it (or paint freely). You do not have to be a good draftsman or writer if you want to do it yourself (bar graphs and amateur analysis are enough). You do not have to see or read your work, but it is usually more productive if you get someone else's views and reactions. You can feel free to be creative as the stories and pictures do not describe the actual situation. You can do whatever you want. You can present things in any way just because you feel right. You can write down what you need to feel comfortable with. Be careful and scared. By inserting something into this frame, you can explain your concerns to others and, of course, increase the number of metaphors and images that you can use when talking to others. If some areas of history evoke strong negative emotions, it could indicate that you need to find a positive way to deal with similar feelings in real situations. If you think someone in the story is critical or harmful, you may need to develop ways to look at those people more compassionately. Over time, you will become aware of cultural assumptions and expectations - what you should and shouldn't do (but may not be the custom of others).

WHY DO YOU IMPROVE YOUR MEMORY?

RECOGNIZE THE POSSIBILITY OF MEMORY

Your memory train, just like any other human teacher. With the right techniques, you can teach memory precisely what you want. You can improve yourself through training and practice, just like playing an instrument or speaking a foreign language. Memory training techniques only work by developing the Brain's natural capabilities.

Starting pointless memory training is like a goalless journey. Identify areas of life that would benefit from a stronger memory. When you focus on them, you get incentives to learn.

BUILD UP TRUST

A lack of trust in your memory paralyzes it and blocks the information it contains. Training ensures that you can access information quickly and accurately. Improvements are generated by yourself. The more memory you use, the better the performance. The higher the storage performance, the higher the utilization. You will find that this improves not only your self-confidence but also your social skills. You can remember your name and the date of your life accurately and efficiently.

IMPROVE RESEARCH SKILLS

Memory training doesn't help you understand new information better, but you can save it and retrieve it correctly. It increases your chances of getting data from your exam quickly and accurately. Instead of finding trouble, you can test your skills, enjoy the exam, and get better results.

WORK MORE EFFICIENTLY

Improving memory improves work efficiency. For example, you can spend less time looking for facts and checking appointments. With complete and accurate information, you can speed problem-solving and decision-making, memorize the names of colleagues, and customers, and improve relationships between work and customers.

SOME TIPS TO SUPPORT YOUR MEMORY

Memory plays a vital role in the Brain and parts of the body. So, if you want to maximize your memory potential, you need to take some simple support measures to keep your body healthy.

LAY THE FOUNDATION STONE

Most people assume that their memory works very quickly with unprecedented accuracy and at any time and in any situation. This laissez-faire attitude leads to inconsistent memory performance. As with other parts of the body, memory must be kept constant over long periods to maximize its potential. The first step in building a solid foundation for memory training techniques is to understand the importance of conscious efforts to maintain awareness.

EAT WELL

Do not underestimate the power of eating as a good memory enhancer. The neurotransmitters that control the ability to exchange information between neurons must be maintained appropriately. The Brain is susceptible to oxidation, so antioxidants are needed. These include foods that are rich in vitamin C, vitamin E, carotenoids, and selenium. Other brain enhancers are fatty acids, especially omega-3 fatty acids: b vitamins and certain minerals. To increase your intake of these nutrients, eat as much fresh food as possible, and avoid cooking. Ginkgo balboa, as a supplement, is believed to improve blood flow to the Brain.

TRAIN YOUR BODY AND MIND

Your physical health plays a vital role in your mental performance. The Brain consumes 20% of the oxygen intake, but only 3% of the total body weight. Improving blood flow through cardiovascular training provides essential oxygen that directly affects brain performance. The exercise should be of moderate intensity. So, do not hold your breath. Aim at least 20 minutes three times a week.

REDUCE STRESS FACTORS

Training your memory improves both your efficiency and your skills, but it's essential to avoid exaggeration. Do not try to do many tasks at the same time. Take control of your life and learn time management techniques to control it.

If you tend to exaggerate naturally, know to say no to people. Relax at home or work with stress-relieving techniques such as simple relaxation exercises and meditation. If you are out of the world and have fun, you should have a little time for yourself every day. Spend relaxing days with family and friends every day and plan regular vacations.

PAY ATTENTION TO THE RHYTHM OF LIFE

The energy level relates to temperature. So, if you monitor the weather, you can see the biorhythm and thus the storage capacity. High-temperature stories usually reflect high energy levels. Check the temperature 3 hours a day and plot the results in a graph. Do this for a week and usually record when the optimal time has come.

SLEEP WELL

Sleep is generally essential for good health, and lack of sleep can lead to mental disorders. Rest plays a vital role in memory consolidation. The same area of new tasks performed during the growing season continues to process information while you sleep. Sleep enables the Brain to store additional information in memory for future use. Therefore, a good night's sleep is essential for a healthy life.

You can remember some of this information for years. For example, an unforgettable birthday, but no other memories last longer than a week. Think of your long-term memory as a library full of books. Some books read more than others, which makes it easier to remember the book you submitted. Some experiences can never forget more than others because they think more in long-term memory. Chapter 5 describes short-term memory. Library check-out table. There are several books in front of you, but you may not be able to remember this information for a long time.

DISCOVER THE IMPORTANCE OF CHILDHOOD MEMORIES

Retrieving reminders before the age of three is often tricky due to poor language skills. If not, how do you talk about what you did that day? And if you can't figure out what you did, how can you add it to a long-term library shelf? Another difficult reason to remember our childhood memories is that our Brain is not yet fully developed at this point. Let's talk about Kaaba. This area plays a vital role in the synthesis of memory and does not develop until the age of two. It is challenging for young children to combine their experiences and transfer them to a long-term memory library.

Take a stroll along memories road to remember your childhood memories. Flick through your photo album to trigger Happy Holidays and read old birthday cards and letters that you exchanged with loved ones. Sometimes it is important to remember how happy you were. Do not keep photo albums in hard-to-reach places such as the attic. Instead, keep the album in a prominent location. Place it for regular access to the bookshelf. Not all memories are reliable. As the name suggests, bad memory is the memory of an event that has never occurred or the decoration of an event that happens. This outbreak is most common in childhood memories. You may remember an unprecedented event like a rabbit when you were young. You can also have a memory that lists the event that occurred. For example, if you had a dog as a pet, you could remember that you and your dog chased a rabbit in a nearby field. But your parents can point out that you lived in a busy city with no nearby areas.

USE THE POWER OF HAPPY MEMORIES

Emotions play an essential role in memory. We may remember that as a child, we spent all the time and spent the summer in the local pool. Other memories that preserve because of a vivid snapshot to create the instance. It may be a surprisingly happy event, but it can also be shocking. Do you remember when you first heard about Diana's death? What did you do when the September 11 bombing reported? Most people, though familiar, recognize these memories in minute detail. Why? Flashlight memories are emotional memories. As a result, trivial events suddenly become more meaningful, and we remember the unimportant information. However, placing an event does not mean that all the details you remember are correct.

SOME TIPS TO IMPROVE YOUR MEMORY

Here are some tips on how to focus on beautiful memories:

THINK HAPPY

Positive thinking can make a difference in your life. In my childhood memories, I seduce the event as I get older instead of looking at it from a positive perspective. It can be the result of subsequent life experiences such as stressful events. But do not let it happen. Think about how an event made you stronger and better instead of letting yourself down. You can also think about why people did what they did.

SCRAPBOOKING IS NOT A DIFFICULT TASK

It is easy to forget a great vacation. Over time, I have to take care of my daily work. Some people keep tickets for events they have visited, brochures, and postcards from places they have seen, or coral and flower stumps from their favorite parks and walks. You can add all these souvenirs to your scrapbook. If you are a little creative, you can buy fantastic books and resources.

HAVE A SNACK

Remember a relaxing sunny day where you can spend the day in the park without going to school. Eating is an excellent trigger for happy childhood memories, as taste and aroma remind you of certain events. If you do not have enough family or childhood friendship, you may get angry at what you ate earlier.

LEARNING PROCESS

Learning something new is a three-step process:

1. Encoding refers to how information is in memory.

2. Memory is a way to monitor messages.

3. If necessary, you can access the data via the entry.

CODING TIPS

IMAGINE

If you need to remember a list of new words, create a visual image in your head instead of repeating the words in your head. When attending a party, do not just think of the person's name. Think about what people are wearing and remember where they were when you met them. All of these visual cues trigger memory when you later need to remember the person's name.

DEEPEN

It's easier to remember something new when you look at what a word looks like or what it sounds like when you look at something superficial or flat. Try to remember as best you can. But this method doesn't help at all. Instead, think about what you mean and rhyme with it. It will be unforgettable to show people more meaningful information.

TO ORGANIZE

"I've said it a lot, why do not you remember it?" Everyone knows this feeling. But you can change that. Create a framework for organizing new information. When reading, think of the framework, and attach what you have read to the framework. It will help you remember what you have read many times.

CREATE A CONNECTION

Link new information with what you already know. Do not only think carefully about what details you learn but also how and how you can link them. As you learn new historical facts, think about what you are used to and connect new recognized historical facts. This process, known as semantic linking, helps you to retrieve the information later.

TIPS FOR LONG-LASTING MEMORIES

Use the tips below to remind you where you left the information. This way, your memory will not be lost.

CONTEXTUALIZATION

When you listen to information, you can release your memory. If you can't remember anything, hear the statement first or return to where you read it. At work, return to the room you were in and re-create the scenario to trigger your memory. If your friend gives you essential information, go back to the cafe or restaurant you spoke.

REMEMBER YOUR CONDITION

You can also quickly identify information based on how you feel about it. If you feel good when you first hear about a new project you've involved in, think about it.

TO TRAVEL

Traveling is the combination of new information and mental images of familiar ones, is a trick that some storage professionals use. Example: Suppose you just woke up and see the John Travolta poster in the closet. You loved Grease in the movie. When entering the bathroom, there is an unfinished school project (model of the Eiffel Tower) in the middle of the floor. You sleep in the living room and watch your brother spill pasta sauce on the sofa.

PROCEDURAL MEMORY

Procedural memory refers to skills that are acquired automatically. You no longer have to think about writing a letter or tying a tie. Your Brain remembers what to do without taking any steps. As a result, it is often difficult to list every step. The problem is how to learn new things. It's a procedural note, and you do not have to think twice? For example, you can discover a new language or complete a dish. The next section contains tips on how to transfer this detail into long-term memory.

PRACTICE FOR PERFECTION

I heard someone say, "Practice has to be perfect." The statement contains a lot of truth. When you do something repeatedly, you train both your Brain and your muscles to learn. Athletes use this muscle memory to "remember" things like cycling and skating and automatically perform actions. Applicable statements are important because if you do not learn the right thing first, the body must first understand the wrong way before it can learn a new and better way to do something. Think about how you hold a pencil. I remember that my teacher was very strict with all the students. If you only have one pen, you have a problem. I am particularly concerned with how to hold a pencil, and I feel strange how to keep a pencil. It also applies to many other activities.

For example, if you enjoy skiing and choosing a lesson, you may be surprised by poor posture and body shape even after skiing for years. Teachers should try to change their form rather than teaching beginners. It is because the muscles do not have to store a specific ski method and must learn the correct shape. The next time you know something new, make sure it's the right way for the first time. So, you do not have to learn twice.

The power of reward in improving memory is known as the law of effectiveness. This law is simple. If you learn something new, you are more likely to repeat the action that triggered your learning. As a child, these rewards can be great results for gold stickers or exams. For adults, this can be praise from relatives or even work promotion. The validity law has another dimension. If you learn something new and get negative things like criticism or disappointment, you are less likely to repeat this action.

Reward yourself! Gold stars and colorful stickers found in the classroom. If you want to learn something new, set up a reward system. Divide the information into smaller parts and give yourself a "sticker" each time you know the role successfully. When you have completed the task, use the rewards that you have set (new clothes, short breaks). A treat doesn't have to cost money. It could be a special day with friends. The goal is to train the Brain, absorb information, and create incentives that connect positive emotions with the learning process. This method not only makes learning more enjoyable, but it also helps you to remember information much longer.

When you look at the rewards and photos of the event, you can remember the information you received as an extra. Many famous athletes do little routines of what they do before the game. Maybe you tie the threads in a certain way or sleep in a uniform the night before the big game. One of the major league ice hockey players put a hockey stick in the toilet before the game. Such superstitions are not uncommon for athletes. While these routines rarely help establish a lasting connection in memory, some people find that repeating regular exercises helps reduce anxiety about actual results or activities.

TRAINING IN YOUR SLEEP

Sleep is a great booster when you learn. When you rest after learning, the information known is amplifying. Do you remember your school days? Do you remember these multiple-choice tests? They look straight-forward but can be very confusing if multiple-choice seems the right answer. Many everyday situations can confuse people. For example, you can forget whether you switched off the stove on the way to the door. Sleep not only improves memory, but it also reduces mistakes when working on tasks. When you sleep, your Brain uses this time to load real and information and separate it from false information. As a result, it is not only updated but also less confusing and forgotten whether the stove was on or not. When musicians try to learn music, they do not just play songs repeatedly. When every musician plays music frequently, the muscles learn to move, but the distraction in the middle of a piece makes it difficult to record and continue playing. Some people have to start over because they can't play at random points in the music.

You do not have to be an excellent musician to use musical techniques. I get nervous when I must learn something new or do something. At a presentation at work. Focus your attention on what you need to do and involve the Brain. First, remove the distractions. You can keep the display on your head instead of repeating it out loud. Consider the various questions that your employees may ask. Finally, consider the answers to these questions in the middle of your presentation. Then continue where you left off and continue production.

TIPS TO IMPROVE YOUR SHORT-TERM MEMORY

There are several ways to improve short-term verbal memory for a better brain:

TIME IS ESSENTIAL

Hearing information affects how well you remember it. Suppose you remember the story at the top of the list instead of the word in the middle of the list, you can try more. It is known as the primacy effect. If someone gives you a long list of tasks, break them up into many plans, and avoid the "slump" in the middle of the list.

REDUCE DISTRACTIONS

Irrelevant thoughts are the disability or another distraction in the region. If they ignore the content of short-term memory, they quickly deteriorate and are lost forever. Minimizing the distraction is essential for the effective use of working memory. Background noise also affects the amount of material you can store. The silence makes it easier to remember the right short-term words. If you are trying to remember important information, reducing music can be helpful.

CONCENTRATE ON ONE THING

Activities that need to draw attention from one thing to another can speed up the process of forgetting. Switching and multitasking can be overwhelming and even forget the simple things. If you are up the stairs: "What have you done here?" If you do many things at the same time, you cannot do one thing well. To reduce this, do one task at a time. It makes it easier for you to remember things at work and home.

KNOW YOUR LIMITS

Think of bite-sized blocks of information to avoid memory overload. It is more important to remember the information you need to remember than to keep an eye on the latest news and prove to be your next memory champion. Repeating the information, you need to remember will help you remember what you need. However, there are two things to consider:

LENGTH CALCULATION

he length of a word makes a big difference in how easy it is to remember. Check out these words: fridge, hippo, Mississippi, aluminum. It is easier to forget than words that are easy to repeat, such as baths, clocks, spoons, and fish. The longer it takes to duplicate or rehearse, the more difficult it is to learn. It is called the word length effect. Long names are hard to remember. To improve your memory in the long term, ask more than just listening to the list.

SOUND IS IMPORTANT

Remembers a list of clearly distinguishable words (bass, clock, spoon, fish, mouse, etc.) and not a list of frequently heard words (rhythmic words such as people, cats, cards, mats, cans, hats). It's painless. If things sound the same, you are more likely to get confused and forget what you need. Therefore, when trying to get a shopping list, do not group the items by category (dairy, meat, bread) and not alphabetically.

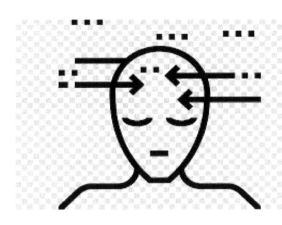

Whatever you do when you survey the area, you will not only learn to read but also remember what you read whenever you need it. Being able to remember without checking details is an excellent benefit for all students. Universities can place very high demands on reading a single course. So, when you have most of the information you need, make your textbooks more efficient and your exams and routine tasks more efficient. Think about what you can prepare. For the first time! This chapter briefly describes how to do this.

Think about the difference between writing and presenting in a newspaper or textbook. The newspaper edited and designed so that it is easy to read. Most newspaper articles organized according to the "pyramid" approach. The first paragraph (above the pyramid) will be the main point of the story, and in the next section, we will add more details and create related topics to fill the pyramid. Read all the headlines and the first few paragraphs to understand the news of the day better. If you are interested in the details, read on.

TO SUMMARIZE THE SKIMMING PROCESS:

1. If you have a title or heading, rewrite it as a question. That is the purpose of your reading.

2. Check all subheadings, images, and graphics. These help to identify important topics in the text.

3. Read the introductory section, overview, and questions at the end of this chapter carefully.

4. Read the first sentence of each paragraph. You will always find important ideas here.

5. Evaluate what you got from this process. Can you answer the questions at the end of this chapter? Can I intelligently participate in class discussions on class materials?

6. Write a summary of what you learned while skimming.

7. Use this assessment to determine if you need a full reading.

READ QUICKLY WITHOUT READING SPEED

The author's headings, subheadings, first sentence, and other tips can help you quickly understand the content of the chapter. However, a few words in this chapter focus on what is essential and what is not. Some things can help you ignore them. Knowing when to accelerate, slow down, skip, and focus can help you read faster and more efficiently. Mathematics, economics, and science texts require a slightly different treatment. You need to follow the steps outlined, but with some significant additions. Do not proceed to the next section unless you fully understand the concepts contained in the various charts and graphs and master the previous quarter. If you have a sample problem, make sure you understand the concepts given by solving issues related to the extent you are reading. If you still do not understand an important idea or equation, start over. However, do not continue. It just wastes time. "Trial and error" are a recognized method of scientific research. However, it is essential to try it out and provide the information. In other words, clearly state where you are going and what you learn from each mistake. Trial and error are appropriate, but much more critical than merely applying the same analysis (solution, conclusion) to a slightly different problem and requiring a real understanding.

MEMORY TRAINING TECHNIQUES

Memory training techniques take full advantage of the natural characteristics of memory. You can order information in various ways using the methods described here. You can use them alone or in combination, depending on what you learn.

INFORMATION ORGANIZATION

Minimize losses and increase efficiency. It is essential to organize the information you receive. Splitting or arranging information into simple patterns is an easy first step in data collection. Simply put, if the Brain is somehow actively involved in processing the data, it is more likely to remember it correctly. Motivate your mind to work more efficiently; the data must be focused on using visions and other sensations and converted into more memorable forms.

IMPROVED CONCENTRATION

Focusing is an essential practice when using storage technology. Compare the memory of a TV show that you saw when you did something at the same time with the memory of a program that was entirely focused. The first case is more accurate and less detailed than the second case. Imagine being asked to learn to concentrate more later. Listen to the radio and answer your friends' questions. This process of checking information after first learning is also essential for improving memory.

USE THE SENSES

Seeing and listening are sensations that commonly used in learning. Develops, seeing, and hearing to make it sharper. Artists are more used to seeing things in more detail and from different perspectives, so they can "see" 30%

more than the average. Make a conscious effort to notice the small parts to improve your senses. For example, spend a day observing the color, nose, and ear types of your neighbors. Listen carefully to their voices - do they have the accents and phrases that they like?

LOCATION USE

Think about how you can mentally go back in time when trying to lose something and remember where you came. It is what your Brain does naturally and is the key to the essential skills of memory training. The "travel" technique uses routes that pass through a known number of locations.

IMAGE CREATION

The basis of all memory training is to create mental images from the learned information. The most memorable thing is that it is rare. Decorate your photos according to the principles of image creation to make them unique and unforgettable. The more you pay attention to the details, the brighter the picture becomes.

USE OF THE ASSOCIATION

Your Brain loves building a repertoire of related information and making connections between data. When the Brain receives new information, it looks for similar things in long-term memory so that it can "understand" what it is. It happens quickly and is not a conscious process. Creating associations improves your memory. By actively creating personalized links for the Brain to connect, you can do some work in your memory and restore it later.

INFORMATION STORAGE

Organizations are the key to properly managing information in many areas of life. The library is a good example. Without a sorting and coding system for organizing books, the library would not work at all. Most offices have efficient filing systems, and all the information you need later is stored in folders in the filing cabinet. The storage technology also takes this into account when receiving new information. For example, create a framework for patterns, locations, etc., and save the data in future storage. It enables the memory to process and store information so that it can recall as efficiently as possible.

IMPROVE DAILY MEMORY

The ability to regularly remember what you need is invaluable. Having this critical information at hand not only increases your confidence and efficiency but also saves time.

SAVE YOUR PIN AND PASSWORD

If possible, use an available date such as your relative's birthday to store your PIN. When you use your password and PIN together, you use words and numbers that you already remember. A friend's house number or zip code. Or use the numbering system image and another image associated with the password. In both cases, create a story that links the image to something that you need to access (e.g., an ATM).

MEMORIES OF EVERYDAY WORK

Mental notes help you remember the tasks of the day. To plan 4-5 days, use travel techniques to plan 4-5 trips. Use the principles of imaging to create a mental picture of each task and insert it into your day trip. For example, if you need dry cleaning, imagine clothes that dance with music and songs. If you need to complete the task at a specific time, add a digital image using any numerical system. Fill out the notes in a few days and save them. If new jobs arise, add them at the end of your trip. You should review your project regularly. Move your head three times a day to make sure nothing is behind you.

MAINTAIN A MENTAL PLANNER

Most people rely on entirely written or computerized planners to organize their monthly hours. Neither system is perfect. Keeping the planner on your head can be very convenient and time-efficient. The learning planner helps you make quick decisions when you make appointments and other arrangements. The basis of the mental planner is travel technology. Initialization can take some time, but once the system set up, it is relatively easy to perform updates.

CREATE A PLANNER

If you are a three-month planner, you need to create three trips (one for each month) and one stage for each day of the month. Take certain breaks at level 10 and level 20 to determine the individual days for each trip. Use three rides in rotation. Create a picture for each planner entry and insert it in the appropriate place. For example, with an 18-day appointment at the dentist, your vision is for the dentist to hit the entire chair. Paste the image on line 18. If you need to add more time, add the corresponding image from the numerical system.

TECHNOLOGY EXPANSION

If it is easy to work on three trips, you can expand the planner to create more trips. Six months or one year is probably enough. You can keep the same imaginary route every year. Start each month with an essential photo of the month. If it is more convenient to use it for three months, you can write down the dates that are older than three months and add them to your trip later.

SPEAK IN PUBLIC

Public speaking is a challenging perspective for many people. You can do this naturally and engagingly by learning to remember some crucial points in your speech, presentation, or play.

PLAN WHAT YOU WANT TO CONVEY

One of the best ways to create a speech or presentation is to map it. Write down the keywords first, and then add the related items that you want to create. This method makes the transmission more natural instead of writing every word. However, if you are going to write your speech entirely or at least linearly, add headings so you can choose keywords.

A MEMORY OF THE LANGUAGE

Remember your speeches and presentations using travel techniques. It is also useful for the timely delivery. For example, if you are planning a 20-minute speech without notes, search for 20 keywords, and take 20 steps. Take one keyword at a time, create a picture, and add one at each stage. If you want to add more information, use Statistics, images of the required numerical system and add them to the appropriate level. Practice your speech to make sure you meet your timing goals. Your language will be a little different every time you grab it, so it sounds fresh.

LEARNING LINE AND QUOTE

If you need to learn theatre lines or read poems or quotes, you can learn the keywords in a fixed order, just like you can in that language. But since we must complete the words, we have to go one step further. We use travel technology to rehearse the line and continue to deliver critical points. Next, you must go through the names to fix minor heart problems. If there are areas that are difficult to remember, take a photo that is easy to remember.

SKILL IMPROVEMENTS

You can apply memory training techniques to a variety of skills that you use in your daily life, from recording information about sports and games to learning languages. Also, the learning experience is fun.

IMPROVE READING

Reading is what we all do - for work, joy, or learning. But most of us cannot read as efficiently or effectively as possible. As a result, we do not remember what we wanted. One way to speed up reading and make the material more memorable is to turn books and articles into mind maps. You must do this from the start, read analytically, and question the order and hierarchy of the information. Organize the story and add it to your mind map.

MEMORY OF FACTS

Fact files and diagrams:

If you can remember facts and maps, improve your general knowledge. Very useful if you want to take part in quizzes and competitions. Create images from every piece of information and link them with associative techniques. For example, if you are going to remember that Michael Douglas won the Oscar in 1987, take a picture from 1987 and attach it to Michael Douglas, who owns the Oscar statuette. The most important thing is to create a fantastic image and save relevant information.

LEARN SPORT

Time and attention are increasingly devoting to both the mental and physical aspects of athletic performance. Memory is a great way to speed up learning as it helps you build good habits from the start. When learning new techniques such as tennis shots and golf swings, the technical aspects divided into essential points. Create a simple, vivid picture for each of these points. For example, if you need to keep your head motionless on tennis serve, imagine wearing a ruff to keep your head steady. Create a trip (probably at the gym) in which essential points saved one after the other. When you start the game, the image of each point crosses your head.

PLAY CHESS

Chess is a technical and strategic game. Opening and closing movements can be learned and used, with previous games remembered as a precedent for future games. To learn chess movements, you must first understand the standard chess notation. Learn these movements with travel techniques, phonetic letter techniques, and your preferred number system. Create a mental picture for each activity, design a trip, and paste the picture on every stage. The full opening may require a journey of 50 steps. To remember whether your hand is black or white, mentally color the image black or white.

IMPROVE CARD SKILLS

If you can remember the card, you have an advantage in the game. Especially if you need to remember what has already played, use the numbering system to create pictures with numbers from 1 to 10. Each picture card has its vision. Create a composite image of the two components for each card. That is, the three clubs could be handcuffs that swing the golf club. To remember the pecking order, create a trip in 52 steps and place the cards in the order in which they come out.

LEARN A LANGUAGE

You can learn vocabulary as the name storing techniques. You can use this technique for words in any language. The most important thing is to listen to the story and then make the association. Create a picture from a foreign language sound and attach the image to the word in your mother tongue. The German language for newspapers is, for example, the newspaper. To remember, you could imagine someone you know reading a newspaper, dropping his tongue and calling it Simon (Si). Visualize this scene in the newspaper section to improve the picture.

SUCCESSFUL EXAM

The memory plays a vital role in academic performance. Improving your memory not only increases your chances of success in the exam but also helps your Brain develop good habits. The more effectively you learn, the more efficiently your memory works.

USE OF MEMORY AIDS

There are several ways you can approach your study to improve your memory of information. 30% of people hear learners - they prefer to hear rather than read. If you want to learn by listening, record some information on tape or minidisc. Play for yourself at different times of the day, for example, during a car ride or before bedtime, just before bedtime. Another technique is the use of flashcards. Write the question on one side and answer it on the other. You can give the card to someone else to help you learn or change the order in which you use the menu to understand information. It will help you remember the exam if you can ask the questions in any order.

STORAGE OF LARGE AMOUNTS OF INFORMATION

The key to learning large amounts of information is to reduce it to a manageable amount. Mind mapping uses keywords for this. It also provides a way to organize the information logically and comprehensively so that the links and related information are specific. Only the mind map keywords need to save. Then the mind map automatically leads you to the relevant area.

THE REMAINDER OF THE FACTS

You can use travel techniques for several facts, including several historical events and the structure of flowers in biology. For example, if you get to know nine planets in the solar system, you first create an image of each world. In other words, Mercury is a thermometer, and Earth is a bargain of Earth. Create a nine-step journey, a stage for every planet. The travel location must be thematic and preferably in a familiar place. In this case, you may be in a fictional spaceship. The next step is to insert the picture into the trip.

STORAGE AND RETENTION OF CALLBACKS

Up to 80% of all information learned lost within 24 hours. Reviewing data is essential for high retention and good recall. Doing this at the right time will reduce the total number of reviews required.

CONFIRMATION OF INFORMATION

For better learning, new information needs to check before the level of memory gets too low. In the first 24 hours, the Brain plays with further information and is bound to exist data. In other words, this time, it is relatively easy to remember. Once this process is complete, the recall level drops quickly. To prevent this, you should check the information regularly. In this way, the Brain can continue to access new information, evaluate it, and remember it in detail.

PLAN

Written planning can integrate learning by regularly requesting information. It is particularly essential for studying, but necessary for information that you want to keep for a long time. The best time to check the information is 1 hour after the first learning. Then you have to check it every one day, one week, three months, and finally every six months after your first degree. Mark this data in the planner and make it part of your action plan.

SET NEW GOALS

Maintaining a high memory strengthens your confidence in your memory and encourages you to continue your learning path. When storage technology becomes part of your life, you can spend quiet time looking at information or remembering new information. It will be a habit, not a chore. If you spend more time reflecting and remembering, you want to try new challenges. Setting these high goals can update your action plan.

USE A STORAGE AID

In addition to transferring information to memory, you may also need to share it with others. Then another storage aid is installed. These are particularly useful when used in combination with storage technology.

WRITE A LIST

Lists are part of everyday life for many. They can be used to remember some important things or to organize work or leisure activities a day, a week or a month ago. Not only does it help you feel that you are in control of your life, but the process of writing the list itself helps your memory. In many cases, it is enough to remember and write something down.

LIST REUSE

Some lists can use several times a year. A good example is a vacation list that lists everything you need to bring. Save time and fear in desperate times before departure and avoid irritation if you forget to use insect repellants on your way to your destination. Keep the list for reuse in a safe place. For example, save your vacation list in a notebook and the names and addresses you need when writing a postcard. All types of plans that are maintained or written might lose their value if they did not keep up to date. Regularly review the list of items as needed and add or remove items as necessary to make a list available.

RECORD THINGS ON PAPER

A household address book is a great way to keep and maintain critical information when other members of your household need access. Planners and individual organizers can combine the functions of address books and notebooks. It is a great way to monitor birthdays, anniversaries, meetings, and dental appointments.

ORGANIZATIONAL INFORMATION

It is a sensible way to keep an eye on yourself at home in an efficient filing system. It is combined with a planner or personal Organizer; it can remind you of quarterly bills, car maintenance, and more. The logical structure of a filing system is likely to be alphabetical, by date or subject, and probably essential. Some people use separate boxes for household accounts, cars, etc. If you have "pending" files, check them regularly.

EXCHANGE OF INFORMATION

When more than one person needs to access the information, it's usually best to write it down somehow. In the office, a wall-mounted mop is a precious way to remind your team of schedules and tasks. In addition to tracking progress, the board serves as a central point for building relationships between groups. At home, the fridge and bulletin board notes can help keep your family organized. Coordinating time together as a family is comfortable with a family calendar in which the entire family participates in family social and extracurricular activities. It also teaches young members to take responsibility for their lives.

LEAVE A RECORD

It is easy to forget what I said at the meeting. It may take a few minutes, but please note if you do not have an official record. The memo is displayed so that you can read it later. Some people find a small tape recorder or dictation machine useful but must ask for permission before it can use.

USE DIGITAL STORAGE

The computer software that stores names, addresses, meeting reminders, and more are common and can include for free on some operating systems. Many programs can set to warn future appointments. An electronic screen display that is compatible with "sticky notes" made of paper is practical. They have the advantage that they do not get stuck and lose valuable lists and memories.

USE AN ELECTRONIC ORGANIZER

Most of us have computers at work or home. These are great ways to save lists, calendars, and other storage aids. Handheld devices, often referred to as PDAs (Personal Digital Assistants), use storage aid functions.

In addition to transferring information to memory, you may also need to share it with others. Then another storage aid is installed. These are particularly useful when used in combination with storage technology.

WRITE A LIST

Lists are part of everyday life for many. They can be used to remember some important things or to organize work or leisure activities a day, a week or a month ago.

KEEP MEMORY ACTIVE

If you train your Brain and keep your memory active, your memory will grow stronger with age. You can do things you have never thought of, e.g., language and musical instruments.

PLAY CROSSWORD PUZZLES AND WORD GAMES

Exercises that keep your memory and Brain active require some mental effort. Crossword puzzles and word games are great because they remind you of words that you may not use regularly. It promotes more use and makes it more transparent. You can also improve mentally by buying books and newspapers in a familiar foreign language. As you read, think of words you do not understand.

USE OF MENTAL ASTHMA

If you can, train yourself to do simple calculations in your head. For example, you can sum up the cost of items in a shopping cart before checking out, or split a restaurant check into several people in your head. You can check the result on the calculator at any time, but you can increase the efficiency of your chair with a simple calculation. So, we learn to rely on estimates rather than calculators.

STAY INTERESTED

Apply the developed memory to your interests. For example, if you want to learn chess, join a local club. Increase the amount of material you learn by keeping the technology under development up to date. The Internet, in particular, can open up a whole new world of information. Continuous learning keeps your memory active and more information provided to absorb it. Reading is an integral part of this process. Read as often as possible. Change the type of book or magazine you read to cover as much material as possible. You are always more likely to remember more exciting information than a dull, uninteresting story. Still, it is common to read something in new areas to expand your memory and interest.

If you have trouble remembering names or faces, do not think you are unique. The 14 storage tasks keep people busy, from placing important data to reading and learning, regardless of where you put it or whether you did it. Four of them relate to identity. The next technique is to avoid that embarrassing cocktail party guff's. It is supposed to prevent the properties of stories and photo series.

LOOK CLOSELY

When you meet someone, look at their face and pay special attention to some great features. Does this person have a big nose? A huge earlobe? Dimple? Big and beautiful blue eyes? Cracking chin? Mole? How do you play card comb? It doesn't have to be incredibly ugly or beautiful. It only differentiates people from the rest of the room. As soon as you unlock it, stop staring. Use your imagination. Let's decorate and highlight it. Make the big nose as big as the toucan's beak on the head. The dimple must be the same size as the crater. A large earlobe should hang on a person's shoulder. Do not assume that everyone you see needs to use this technique. It's easier to jog memories with specific clues. Can you know the person's spouse at the party? Do you remember his name? Voila! Suddenly you remember her name. What if you recognize someone and do not know why? Think about where you know him instead of focusing on one person or face. We remember people in certain situations, and meeting them outside of this situation can lead to difficult problems. Perhaps the same guy had a full tank of fuel once a week for several months, but suddenly a baseball game confused him. If you remember working for a gas station, you could probably recognize his name.

MAKE SURE YOU HAVE IT

Remember introducing your friend Tony to the first three who arrived at your house for dinner. A minute later, he went to the kitchen to fix the drinks for everyone, and Tony was next to him. "What's the name of the brunette in the mini skirt?" He asked quietly. "Monique," he said. "A bald man?" Asked Tony. "This is Joe," Tony asked, feeling very embarrassed at the end. "What about the other woman?".

The first thing he taught him was to repeat his name. Tony is a handsome guy and doesn't pretend to be the main character in the being their remake. He says his name as part of the greeting - friendly to meet you, Monique. "Joe, hello. It would be better if he heard it." Not only do you know the person's name, the use of such techniques, but you can also check that the name is correct. When you are thinking about links, think of some links that exaggerate between names and functions.

YOU SAY TOO MERELY

Something is more convenient. Do not overlook the obvious before taking an unforgettable photo in the distance. Some names are impressive, and you do not have to work hard. Try "Boomer" Elias's son ("Um, maybe you need to work on Elias"). Your organization can use your knowledge. When Klein speaks German, she works with her favorite little athletes, films, stars, and writers who are associated with job-specific terms. The list of possible partnerships is endless. If such a link is still unthinkable, you can always rhyme. The wallet weighs 1 ton for the wallet, George Spouge, Bert Chad, Freaky Frank, and Ron.

Once you've found these similar sounds and photos, you can link them to an image made up of the person's main facial features. For example, when I approach a man named Vince Dolce (pronounced Dorsey), I found some black bears under his eyes. In my mind, the circle is more significant than the raccoon because I'm used to the technique above. When I heard that his name was Dolce, I immediately thought of it as a "boring sheep" and imagined a sheep that was tired and sleepy and was grazing in a more massive ring under Vince's eyes. Of course, the sheep bothered him, which made him stupid (for Vince). It's about turning a room full of strangers into good and bad people who will never forget!

REMEMBER THE NAME

Many people find it difficult to remember their names. I try all kinds of memories with varying degrees of success, but I'm confident that I do not have to do anything else, especially with the name learning method.

USE ASSOCIATION TECHNIQUES

I feel special when I remember the name of the person I met. In business situations, it is advantageous to be able to name customers or to work with them. In the first minutes after completing a new person, you can use this name to build a close relationship. There is an easy way to improve the memory of words. The key is to use your imagination. The technique of remembering names over time is called an association technique. It has two steps. Create a picture and attach it to a person.

CREATE A PHOTO FROM YOUR NAME

When you hear a person's name for the first time, an associated picture immediately created. First, listen to the associations that come to your mind and learn to use them. These are the associations I remember. For example, the name Julie could promote the image of jewelry, but the words are similar because Bill reminds me of dollar bills. You see a picture of a phone booth in the last name booth and remember the microphone Shin sang. Look at a person's face and attach it to their head to look for unique features.

ATTACHMENT

After meeting the person, we use the principle of image creation to describe the photo taken for the name in detail and attach it to the person. Her picture was Julie's jewel. You can see her wearing a piece of jewelry. Enhance your image by imagining bright and shining eyes. Hear the flickering of her gold chains as she leaves. When you meet the person again and look at their face, you will ask to remind them of the photo that triggers their name.

USE OF SNAIL TECHNOLOGY

The letters represent the introductory slowdown, hear words, use names, and confirm terms. When introducing someone, you usually have little time to implement association techniques effectively. The SLUG technique is a simple 4-step process. When most people forget you, they are briefly named and remembered.

LISTEN, USE, CHECK

You may not be able to come for pick up later unless you ask for the other person's name. Therefore, concentrate on the moment of the first name and consciously record it. Then it is essential to use the new name. If possible, use it three times during the first meeting, immediately after the introduction, during the conversation, and when you say goodbye. A short introduction can identify you by your name. After all, you must remember your name shortly after leaving the company and the next day. About 80% of the new information can forget within 1-2 days without confirmation.

COMBINATION TECHNOLOGY

Both association and SLUG techniques help you remember names. However, you can use both methods together to increase the likelihood that you will remember your name when you meet a new person. Use the SLUG technique while referenced to someone else and use the related methods to assign words to that person during or after a conversation. This way, both the person and name are stored in your memory and can be easily retrieved when you need to use the next meeting or word.

REMEMBER THE WORDS AND LETTERS

Store strings like names, phrases, or lists using one of two simple techniques. The acronym creates a memory trigger while the audio procedure applies an image to a character.

CREATE AN ACRONYM

Acronyms are the old way of storing lists. To create an acronym, take the first letter of each element and put it in a word. For example, the Great Lakes are Huron, Michigan, Superior, Ontario, and Erie. Sort by Huron, Ontario, Michigan, Erie, Superior. The first letter creates the acronym HOMES.

USE EXTENDED ABBREVIATIONS

Extended acronyms take the first letter of a word and use it as the first letter of a sentence word. Useful when you need to view articles in a specific order. A popular acronym for rainbow colors in the right order (red, orange, yellow, green, blue, indigo, purple) is, for example, Richard von York Gabe Battle in Vine.

WITH LANGUAGE TECHNOLOGY

From passwords to license plates, one or more characters displayed in different places. Most letter patterns are not suitable for photography. Therefore, it needs to convert into something that can connect to memory. The Furigana lettering technique uses the Furigana alphabet. It is the international system of English-speaking countries that assigns words to every letter. This term uses to create an image.

IMAGE PERSONALIZATION

The next step is to create an image for each word. For example, the photo is a scale (kg) for K kilos and a whiskey bottle for W whiskey. It is essential to create images that are easy to remember. Please think of the picture. Words and letters returned. To reproduce the text, make the story in the correct order for the photos.

REMEMBER THE LIST

Travel technology is a very versatile and surprisingly powerful way to learn the wrist. You can learn a lot from weekly planner entries to important past exam days.

UNDERSTAND TECHNOLOGY

This technique is probably the oldest known storage aid. It works on the principle of storing information that you need to remember mentally. So, you can take it with you wherever you need it. This technique also uses images and associations to use all of the brain's natural memory tools used to maximize the effect.

TRAVEL DESIGN

Organize the list of items to learn. The route must follow a logical path from start to finish so that you can remember it more easily. The number of travel levels should match the number of elements that need to learn. The vacation list contains six parts, so the move requires six steps. Get a pen and paper to practice your trip once you've decided on a route, place objects at all stages of your journey.

ASSUMPTIONS ABOUT OBJECTS IN THESE PLACES

After inserting each item in the list at its assigned position on the trip, the next step is to use imaging principles to create a stupid scenario for each room. The more bizarre the scenes, the easier it will be to remember. Objects on the vacation list have no particular order and can be placed anywhere in the house. The charge is not mandatory here, but it can be vital if you learn, for example, what to do in a speech. The illustration shows four objects on a vacation list and four fictitious scenarios for four rooms on an example trip.

CHECK YOUR PROGRESS

After pasting the images in these places, let's go back and have fun. If you are satisfied, write the list on another piece of paper and test it. Why did you think for the second time that both the number of recalled items and the recalled speed has improved dramatically? Your self-confidence is more important because you are confident in things. The guesswork is gone. You will find that the information you have learned is correct and complete.

REMEMBER NEW LIST

If you know a list of information that you only need to visit once or twice, you can reuse the trips created for it. Use the new list of trips about a month after the trip ends. However, if you want to learn a plan that you want to keep for a long time, you need to think about a new journey, especially for this one project. Creating a recent trip is not that difficult. As with any mental ability, the more you do it, the easier it will be.

REMEMBER THE NUMBERS

A series of numbers from a credit card PIN to a telephone number is part of everyday life. It's easy to learn how to store numbers. Using numbers to improve your skills develops all aspects of mental performance.

TRY A DIFFERENT SYSTEM

There are two central systems with which numbers can memorize. Number Rhyme and Number Shape System. It's fun and easy to use. It is the base on the rule of combining numbers and photos and creating stories from them. Try both systems to find out which is better. If you choose one, leave it alone. Do not use both methods at the same time and do not exchange between systems.

LEARN THE NUMBER SYSTEM

The Number Lime System is particularly suitable for auditory thinkers who can think, listen, and naturally explain ideas. The first step is to change the numbers 1 through 9 into an image that rhymes with that number. Here's one of the lists, but if you think of words that rhyme yourself, you can learn photos more efficiently.

REMEMBER THE NUMBERS

The next step is to attach an image to the information. There are two different methods. One is a number, and the other is multiple numbers. Suppose a friend recently moved in and needs to remember a new home number to explain the one-digit method. For example, if the number is 3, imagine it in front of a tree. Here the photo is selected as number 3. Imagine

building a wooden house to emphasize that it is a
house number.

THE MEMORY OF SEVERAL DIGITS

The multi-digit number storage method requires
you to create a short story and link the images
for each number. Of course, the photos must
display in the correct order. Imagine the theft
alarm code is 4583. Imagine a story that includes
doors (4 views), honeycombs (5), gates (8), and
trees (3). To link an image to a robbery alarm,
you can look at the scene and imagine a robber
with a mask on his face.

NUMBER SHAPE SYSTEM LEARNING

Those who think visually usually think a formal
numerical system is appropriate. The visual
thinker looks at the photo in his head and notices
what the object looks like. The number format
system works the same way as the number
rhyme system, but the images you create have a
similar shape to numbers instead of rhyming with
numbers. Here is a list of recommended photos.

FORM NUMBER

Next, you need to add an image to the number
you want to learn. Take a picture of each number
and link it in the correct order with the other
users in the story. Suppose you take flight 267

and meet someone at the airport. With the suggested picture, you can imagine a swan (2) (7) with an elephant's trunk (6) playing the saxophone. If you do this in the cockpit of an aircraft, you can remember the number and link it to the flight.

THE MEMORY OF LONG NUMBERS

Most numbers used daily, exceed four digits. By combining your chosen numbering system with travel technology, you can further develop the corresponding numbering system. Numbers with more than four digits are divided into smaller numbers and put on a mini trip. Divide numbers with more than eight digits into at least three sections. Phone numbers are usually the most massive numbers that need to be processed. Suppose your new doctor's number is (414) 555-1678. Use a numbering system of your choice to create and place three stories in the clinic, one for each part of the number. The excursion has a parking lot, a waiting room, and an examination room. When traveling, the images should be used in chronological order so that they can display in the correct order.

CHAPTER 7: NUMERICAL REASONING & VISUAL REASONING AND SPATIAL AWARENESS

NUMERICAL SUITABILITY

Numbers are everywhere! But please indicate that due to math, many of us are afraid. It can be surprising since even babies and animals can register rudimentary counting mechanisms. Everyone has a natural number of talents. It built into our being. We always deal with numbers and use them for mental exercises. Think about it. When we wake up, it is usually because the alarm clock turns off at the set time (time to read and interpret the number). When you buy something, you use numbers to quantify its value. Use the numbers to get the right ratio when preparing your favorite dish according to the recipes in the book. Numerical thinking forms the basis for logic, rationality, reasoning, and proof. When asked if they are good at math, they tend to give negative answers because they fill the memory of the struggle between formulas and fractions, geometry, and trigonometry.

NUMEROPHOBIA

Some people find it challenging to deal with the number of young people. They cannot respond, be it due to fear of school or mental illness. To overcome anxiety, you need to learn, recognize, and continue to overcome. You will be amazed at how quickly your brain reacts to new responses that are aware of persistent fear.

VISUALIZE THE MATH

The visualization of mathematical concepts makes numerical thinking easier. Einstein once claimed that his thinking process triggered by visualization, but he rarely thought. Brain scans must show that the activity to be calculated is not limited to the left hemisphere, but is also present in the visual, auditory, and motor cortex of the brain. Due to the nature of the geometry and the diagrams, graphical skills must also use to understand complex numerical data. Complex numerical data immediately encompass the area of the right temporal lobe. What we do know is that when a math problem observed, it becomes more transparent and accessible, and the brain can later remember that knowledge.

IMPROVE ARITHMETIC

Constant practice is the key to improving your numerical skills. If you are serious about strengthening general mental arithmetic, do not rely on calculators for now. Of course, a calculator is a convenient and necessary tool. The problem is that most of these parts are somewhat lazy on both sides of the brain. Therefore, if you want to improve your arithmetic skills, do not use the calculator for all the arithmetic calculations required. Another thing to remember is that improving your math skills can give you a significant psychological reward. You feel wise when you get it. The mathematics that goes beyond the necessary calculations, such as Geometry, has powerful visualization capabilities because the mind's eyes use them to solve. The more you practice, the more you concentrate. You will be more focused; it is an essential part of success in life.

VISUAL MATH TRAINING

When you start creating math graphics, different parts of your brain become active, which leads to more extensive brain training. You will also learn to understand the language of mathematics by finding ways to visualize its logical meaning. The truth is that when people presented with large numbers and esoteric symbols, they are distracted by numerical problems. No wonder that adding visual components to your math learning is appealing from the start.

LOGIC FLIES OUT OF THE WINDOW

RULE OF THUMB

Most of us apply heuristic knowledge based on intelligent reasoning rather than the logic known in psychology. It is the natural answer to incomplete information and complex problems. Our brain encoded with these generally efficient rules that can learn or inherited to fill gaps. It leads us to well-founded assumptions and intuitive decisions. In other words, we use common sense. There is only one minor mistake. Most of the time, our brain can give the right answer, but it can confuse us if we do not stop and step back and use logic. But it's easier than you think. The problem is that although we are wrong and biased, we believe that we are right. It is a recipe for trouble. For this reason, psychologists are very interested in the use and effectiveness of heuristics.

NUMERICAL PUZZLE SOLVING

Puzzles are like logic errors but ultimately use the wrong logic. Puzzles are usually vague expressions in a pictorial or allegorical language. They designed to trip you up. So, you need to think carefully to find the right solution. The best puzzles allow your brain to fill missing gaps without correct reasoning and to confuse you with all possible methods. The secret of mathematics is abstract, so it is essential to pay special attention to information that is not important the first time you read it. Some of the "important" information you get may be there so that you won't notice the problem yourself!

ROOM DETECTION

Of course, visual and spatial thinking is critical in memory. Think of a taxi driver navigating a tangle of city streets. But it is also an essential skill in many other professions—visual thinking required for intricate design and layout work areas such as architecture and urban planning. People who work in these areas rely on the ability to represent ideas graphically. If you are planning a day outdoors and need to fill your picnic basket, how do you fit your groceries, dishes, and utensils in a confined space before you start loading?

SEEING IS LEARNING

Unlike other types of thinking (like numerical and verbal thinking), visual thinking is not something that most education systems deal with directly. A separation such as linguistic thinking (language) or numerical thinking (mathematics) is probably not sensible, as already used in various subjects such as art, sports, mathematics, and music. There seems to be almost none. Nourish this unique mental ability. As a result, most people do not learn how to make the most of their visual thinking skills. Some psychologists also suggest that classifying an educational system as defective is an error in the educational system. Visual thinking is a proven way to organize ideas and find consistent solutions to problems. Optical thinking techniques improve memory, focus, organization, critical thinking, and problem-solving.

IMPROVE SPATIAL INTELLIGENCE

Spatial reasoning skills are always required but are usually the result of repetitive tasks such as moving a shopping cart through a supermarket aisle or parallel parking on a familiar driveway. Work with the autopilot. In this way, they do not stimulate spatial intelligence but rely on spatial memory to work on new spaces, shapes, forms, and dimensions. A simple and efficient way to improve spatial intelligence is to do a mechanical 3D puzzle-like Rubik's Cube. Research has also shown that playing video games has a significant impact on general spatial perception. If you are not good at shooting maps or simulating racing cars, there are other easy ways to improve spatial compatibility.

ENHANCE CREATIVITY

From music to drawing, there are many ways to be creative. The benefits of creative brain work include the ability to think across borders, find unique solutions to problems, and even enjoy certain activities. Have fun with regular training. Your working life also benefits from your creative activities.

INCREASE YOUR STRENGTH WITH CREATIVE EFFORTS

Training your brain is not difficult! Creative thinking - where you can find solutions to problems - is a great way to encourage your mind to include information from different sources. It means finding an alternative perspective (abnormal or unique) instead of giving up when the problem seems complicated. Not everyone can be the next Beethoven or Da Vinci, but here are some suggestions on how to develop your creative side.

GET READY

"Chance only supports the prepared mind." A quote by the renowned scientist Lewis Pasteur summarizes what scientists know today by examining brain patterns. Shortly before the problem occurs, different parts of the brain show activation. In other words, the mind is ready and gathers information from other functions to find a solution. When problems arise, solutions rarely come from the air. The answer is often the result of hours and hours of preparation. The next time you have issues, do your homework, and be well prepared. Creative solutions will follow shortly.

OKAY, I WON'T TALK ANYMORE

Talking too much about a problem can ruin the creative process. Studies show that the creative process works best if the plan not spoken continuously. In many ways, innovative solutions are automated processes. Some say that creativity has an unconscious element. You do not have to be creative. The next time you try to be creative, do not talk about it, and let the brain do the work.

LOOK AWAY

Focusing too much on a problem can affect creativity. Scientists have found evidence that if the problem concentrated over a long period, the brain generates excessive amounts of gamma waves with extreme attention. This increase in gamma waves causes mental disorders, but of course, it does not help to solve the problem. So, if you lose your creative atmosphere, it's time to get up and get away from the situation. Do something else unless the activity relates to the issue you want to solve. After a short pause, your brain will recharge when you return.

TIPS TO INCREASE YOUR INTEREST IN MUSIC

Here are some tips to promote the musical side:

SING ALONG

Young children react to the pitch and rhythm of the language. The term mother refers to a loud and humble voice from her. Talk to your baby often. Studies show that babies pick up these pitch patterns and return in the same way. Early communication characterized by imitation of the pace and rhythm of the language. When a mother is tired of a method, so does her baby.

PLAY AND PAY ATTENTION TO MUSIC

Music lessons help students understand the lessons better. Studies have shown that playing musical instruments frees young people from the significant distractions of school and enables them to focus more on the teacher's voice. Playing the tool not only teaches the brain to increase the volume of all sounds but also helps the brain effectively differentiate sounds from related information. When someone learns a musical instrument, they train the mind to extract relevant melodic patterns such as harmonies and rhythms. The brain can use the same functions to filter and record speech and other sounds in the classroom or on the playground.

LISTEN TO MUSIC

Listening to music activates various parts of the brain that are involved in processing attention, memory, information, and emotions. Music can also heal the hearts of adults. Studies have shown that listening to music can speed up cognitive recovery in stroke patients. The patient's verbal memory and attention improve faster than those who only listen to the audiobook. As a bonus, listening to music while your stroke is recovering helps avoid negative moods like depression.

IMPROVE YOUR MEMORY

Studies have shown that adding words to music can significantly improve the memory of people with Alzheimer's disease. The part of the brain associated with memory works more slowly in the amount of the mind with Alzheimer's disease. However, inserting words that you need to remember into your music creates a more robust memory connection than repeating the comments themselves. So, if you know that people with Alzheimer's have trouble remembering their daily chores, add them a list of tasks in the music and sing.

KEEP YOUR BRAIN AT THE PERFECT PITCH

Scientific evidence shows that music training improves memory. Despite educational background and age, musicians tend to remember more information than non-musicians. In other words, playing an instrument activates a part of the brain (cerebral cortex) and improves access to information. Musical education is suitable for scientists. When children exposed to music lessons with complex rhythms and tones, they usually understand reading better than children of the same age who do not take music lessons. But improvement is not the only problem. Psychologists have found that math skills and spatial thinking are also suitable for students taking music lessons. What music helps children use their heads at school? When people listen to music, various systems activated throughout the brain. In addition to working memory, the brain processes musical information about both the left and right brain.

DRAW AND UNLOCK THE CREATIVE SIDE

Drawing a picture increases your imagination. It is essential to find a creative solution to your problem. If you feel sloppy, you can draw something more complicated than a wavy line. Here are some ideas to attract and unlock the creative side.

MAKE A MAZE

Start with a clue. It doesn't have to be profound. In simple cases, it can also be an object. Write your thoughts on paper. Next, let's think about another idea. How can I combine two pictures? Continue until your paper looks like a labyrinth of thoughts and ideas. The maze may not make sense at first. However, if you try a few times, the process will be more straightforward. And you will find that your brain can make more connections between different events that can blow up your creative process.

MAKE CARDS

The next time you need to buy a birthday card, create one. From drawing to drawing to restoring the precious memories you've shared with old photos. You have unlimited options. It is not just a more meaningful way to share your thoughts. You can also be creative by creating cards. Making scrap cards is not what you want. Consider scrapbooking. With all the photos around, you can finally do something. It's a great way to keep memories. If most of your photos are digital, you can do virtual scrapbooking on many online sites and share your pages with family and friends.

DRAW A CARTOON

Comic and graphic novels are a great way to capture your thoughts. Why not draw instead of looking for the right words to describe your feelings today? You may also be surprised! If you dare, you can publish your comic on your blog online and get feedback from your friends. You can also create your manga. Whatever you choose, making this type of diary is a fun way to express your thoughts and be more creative!

MAINTAIN A POSITIVE ATTITUDE

Sometimes "suddenly loses life" or "throws a curveball at you." Crises and problems can suddenly occur at unexpected times. However, you can determine how the issue affects you. Overwhelming issues can lead to stress and anxiety and impair brain function. If you choose to overcome the problem, you will experience superior benefits in your brain.

SMILE THE WAY TO A BETTER BRAIN

"A smile will find someone to smile at you," I remember growing up in that little tolerance, something on the map that my school friend gave me. When I was younger, I liked the idea that a different face made me smile. But a smile makes you feel better, and you may be wondering if it's perfect for your brain. Studies have shown that positive emotions, such as happiness and joy, are closely linked to physical and mental health. In contrast, negative emotions such as worry and sadness can worsen your health. Positive emotions promote health in countries where people cannot meet their basic needs, for example, where they live and what foods they eat. There are other reasons to look at the right side of life! When life is stressful, significant life events can cause stress, but this also enables the accumulation of everyday responsibilities that can be overwhelming. The more you have to take into account, the more pressure you feel. However, the right approach cannot be overwhelmed but can change potentially stressful situations in a variety of ways. Here are some ideas:

ASK QUESTIONS

Instead of saying, "I can't do this" or "It's too difficult for me," try to paraphrase it as a question. Ask yourself, "What can I do?" Or by asking a problem instead of leaving a negative comment, "What can I do?" Instead of recognizing the hurdle, you can change your thinking about the opportunity. For example, when asked to complete a challenging project at work, do not let potential customers know what they need to accomplish. Instead, tasks break down into smaller, achievable goals that are guided by questions. What should I do first? How can I do this first step? And so on.

CHANGE MINUS TO PLUS

It is never too early to think of a harmful situation. You may not have this action at work, but you may have found something useful. Can you spend time with your family or start a project you always wanted but didn't have time? Concentrating on the silver lining in unexpected situations may not always be easy, but it may be difficult.

HAVE A HERO

Imagine someone who inspires others to overcome difficult situations and win. For example, Lance Armstrong diagnosed with cancer, but he didn't stop it. He won the Tour de France for several years in a row. He was the only one to set a record and win seven times.

Inspirational stories like Lance Armstrong are great because they can motivate people to create their own success stories that can share with others.

THINK POSITIVE

What you read can have a more significant impact on your brain than you think. Studies show that reading laughter is enough to change behavior. Even if you try to control what you feel, happy feelings permeate. If you have questions about why you can't skip the steps, read the documentation. It may be time to replace the Whippy Story with a brighter one. Try the following techniques to benefit from positive thinking and optimism.

DO NOT GIVE UP

Even if it doesn't start or the project doesn't work as expected, everyone stumbles on the way. What you do after you fail is essential. Do you feel sorry for yourself and avoid trying again? Or do you sit down and try again? Imagine a story like the Walt Disney story. Remember that life is not the golden path to success. It's an uneven, bumpy road and whether to get up and keep going.

GOODBYE STRESS

Positive thinkers are less stressed than those with negative thoughts. People who receive positive reviews believe in themselves and in what they can achieve. However, if something goes wrong, they will find a way to turn the situation into a good one and quickly find a way to overcome the setback.

CHANGE PERSPECTIVE

You know that feeling. Since something is wrong, I can't stop thinking about it. Rumination is a term used by psychologists to describe the process of trying to solve things in the mind.

Psychologists identify two types of ruminants:

REFLECTION
Reflection is a positive reaction to a problem and leads to finding a solution. Now is the time to identify the problem and develop an action plan to solve it.

BREEDING
Breeding is more harmful and involves strong emotions, such as worries and fears. Breeding means repeating something in your head or playing something with an ambitious (or not ambitious!) listener. Such behavior usually causes stress. Because it only focuses on the negative side of the situation (the "dummy" syndrome), not on what you were thinking about

before, for example, on what you want right now. Then plan a proactive solution to your problem. If you repeatedly play a scene or event in your head or are self-critical, you can simply feel dark. So, do not do it. Sometimes you can be your worst critic. A regular criticism of yourself can affect your mental health and lead to self-fulfilling prophecies. Start believing what you think of yourself (e.g., failure). The next time you want to criticize yourself, stop, and think about what's right in your situation. List all positive answers.

Compulsive regret for something not only takes time but can also lead to more serious mental health problems. If you are always worried, do the following to avoid negative trends.

KEEP AN EYE ON YOUR GOALS

The goal is to solve the problem. Do not upset your heart, and do not get discouraged when you say things like "it doesn't work for me." These ideas are useless and do not help me find a solution. Write down the problem. Then we list two or three things you can do to solve the problem. A written review of the problem (and possible solutions) can make a big difference and prevent dark thoughts from accidentally whirling around in your head. Please be strict.

FIND THE MIDDLE

Sometimes you may need to lower your expectations. It can be impossible to get the perfect answer. Please do not hang around. Find the solution that suits you best. Remember that a healthy brain is a dark, laid-back brain. So, do not waste your spiritual energy and hope to change the past. Finding a workable solution can change the future.

TAKE SOME TIME

Sometimes you must take a break from the problem. Be mental for a while. You can meet your friends and have fun together and not to mention your time problems.

CALL FRIENDS

Seeking help is not a sign of weakness. Do not bear the mental burden of the problem yourself. If you cannot create an action plan to solve the problem, ask a friend for help.

DEALING WITH STRESS AND FEAR

Stress plays a vital role in the development of several severe mental disorders, including depression. One of the interesting questions is why some people are more stressed than others. The answer may link to combat or flight mechanics. If someone gets into a stressful situation, does he avoid it (escape), or does he adapt and try to deal with it (fight/deal)?

Answering this question seems to indicate whether stress can overwhelm you. Studies in mice have shown that those who avoid stressful situations with large, aggressive mice are more likely to suffer from anxiety. In contrast, a person that had found a way to adapt and deal with the case had a healthier brain. Therefore, flight options are not always optimal. Sometimes figuring out how to coordinate and deal with it is less stressful, and in the long run, it is better for your mental health.

UNDERSTAND WHY STRESS KILLS BRAIN CELLS?

Which parts of the brain are most affected by stress? Scientists have found that the hippocampus associated with long-term knowledge and spatial memory suffers the most. It could explain why depression also affects memory. Depressed people may have difficulty receiving new information (this is the responsibility of the hippocampus).

Stress can also cause the brain to contract physically. Studies have shown that high levels of stress can reduce the amount of hippocampus and anterior cingulate cortex associated with stress hormone control. Stress kill - that's what people say, but is this statement correct? Well, some strains are suitable for your brain; others are not. Here are the main reasons why you should avoid stress if you want to keep your brain in top shape:

AVOID SABOTAGE

Know when your actions can disappoint you. Some people can deal with stressful situations in a way that makes the situation worse. Offensive behavior is an example. Quietly expressing emotions about the situation without shouting or stressing is better than being aggressive. Assertiveness means making your claim without harassing or manipulating others. You calm down and clarify your intentions. Another example of self-annoyance is overeating or overeating rather than finding a healthy way to deal with the situation.

LOWER BLOOD PRESSURE

Stress leads to high blood pressure. Scientists have found that in a group of almost 1,000 adults over the age of 65, people with high blood pressure are at increased risk of mild cognitive impairment. It means that these adults have had difficulty concentrating, having difficulty performing simple mental activities, and forgetting things more often.

SLIDE DOWN A SLOPE

If you think something you forget can live with you, think again. Slight cognitive impairment can lead to dementia and Alzheimer's. 15% of people with mild cognitive impairments then fight dementia and Alzheimer's. Studies show that mild cognitive impairment is the strongest predictor of memory loss. In other words, the level of education, e.g., Where you live, male or female, is less critical. It is all the more important to avoid stress on the roof—another reason to spend a weekend relaxing and not being able to work.

Eating has tremendous strength in the brain, from memories of happy childhood memories to relaxation of blunt nerves. But most people probably consider food to be purely functional. It's something you must do to keep moving. Eating is something you can do without much worry. Occasionally with friends in a new fashionable restaurant, sometimes even watching TV. However, this chapter emphasizes how food can transform the brain from childhood to adult life. It is always a good idea to get advice from a suitably qualified doctor before making significant changes to your diet.

FOOD FOR LIFE: UTERINE NUTRITION

Lifestyle changes during pregnancy are usually the last thing a woman has in mind. The only difference a pregnant woman wants to make is to raise her leg and enjoy the relatively quiet final months before the baby arrives. However, choosing the right food can bring significant benefits to both you and your baby's brain. If healthy choices mean a change to you, do it - the minds of you and your baby will thank you.

DESIRE FOR MALT

You may have heard of a woman waking her partner up in the middle of the night, wild goose hunting, and sending an elusive food combination like chocolate dip cucumbers or the store's special nut bread jam. They loved their vacation. The list goes on. Most of the time, these weird demands are just food cravings, but with some food cravings, the brain tells you that you are missing something, like calcium and protein, in your daily food intake. We do not intend to provide a list of essential nutrients needed during pregnancy. Instead, I'm trying to develop the three best brain boosters that can only live when you are pregnant.

MILK - MORE THAN JUST CHILDREN

If you've never had milk, unless you've drunk a few drops of tea or coffee, pregnancy is a time of change. In addition to the apparent benefits of calcium, which strengthens the baby's bones and teeth and improves muscle and nerve function, milk also has other advantages. Pregnant women who drink milk during pregnancy can reduce the risk of Multiple Sclerosis (MS) in their children. Symptoms of MS include fatigue, weakness, and acute or chronic pain. But do you know that MS also affects the brain? Cognitive deficits, such as depression and language problems also occur in MS patients. Pregnant women who drink less than one milk a week are more likely to have a higher risk of developing MS in children. The benefits of milk lead to vitamin D. The next time you are thirsty, drink a carbonated drink and reach for milk (or vitamin D supplements instead - ask your doctor).

IRON IS NOT JUST FOR MUSCULAR PEOPLE

Iron is essential for the baby's brain development and has severe cognitive consequences if the mother does not get enough iron. For example, iron deficiency in a baby growing in the womb causes learning and memory problems later in the baby's life. These negative consequences are often irreversible. So, the takeaway message is to give your baby the best starting point and get enough iron. Most pregnant women get folic acid and iron supplements from their doctors. But you can also get iron from food sources. Red meat is the best source and the largest source of iron. If you are looking for a vegetarian sauce, you can get iron from cereals and legumes. You get the same amount of iron in just a quarter cup of bran.

EAT 1, 2, AND OMEGA 3

Omega 3 is a polyunsaturated fatty acid found in fish and various seeds. Fats are not popular, but polyunsaturated fats are one of the four types of fats that your body gets mainly from what you eat. And your baby needs it to develop his brain. You may be familiar with common omega-3 food sources such as fatty fish (salmon and mackerel) and olive oil. But do you know that you can probably get omega-three from the spices in your kitchen? Some of them are cloves, basil, sage, oregano, and mustard seeds. If your baby does not get enough omega-3 fatty acids from what you eat, he will take them out of his business, which may result in you losing up to 3% of your brain cells.

The news is simple, but 15-20% of women smoke during pregnancy. As I heard, this message is so important that I must repeat it. Smoking during pregnancy carries severe risks for you and your baby:

1. Smoking mothers can give birth to immature, underweight babies.

2. Smoking has consequences in children.

If the baby of a mother who smokes during pregnancy grows, the mental health of her child can have serious consequences. Mothers who smoke during pregnancy are at increased risk of developing psychotic symptoms such as hallucinations and delusions in their teenage years. In the womb, tobacco can affect the brain by influencing impulsiveness, alertness, and even mental development.

RESIST A SWEET IMPULSE

If your area is a food lover, you may think that pregnancy is the time to buy all of your favorite foods, regardless of calories or fat. But before you pay attention to the wind, you should remember the effects on you and your baby.

DO YOU LIKE FOOD?

Pregnant mothers who eat high-fat sweet foods affect the development of the baby's brain. The baby's brain pleasure center became increasingly unresponsive. That means they have trouble saying no. As a result, these children develop the habit of overeating, are prone to obesity, and can show habitual behavior in adulthood. Babies born to their mothers on a high-fat diet during pregnancy are more susceptible to high-sugar foods than mothers who are pregnant on a standard diet.

HIGH SUGAR

Gestational diabetes occurs in up to 10% of pregnancies and is characterized by hyperglycemic women during pregnancy. If a pregnant mother has high blood sugar, her child may be less sensitive to insulin, a risk factor for type 2 diabetes.

FOOD FOR LIFE: CHILD NUTRITION

The good news is that a healthy and nutritious home environment can give a child the first step in life. Many successful epidemics claim that children have the magical combination of nutritional values they need to succeed. Avoid taking supplements unless an official agency approves them (e.g., the British Food Standards Agency or the United States Food and Drug Administration). Many supplements on the market claim to be "vitamins" and not approved by government agencies. Do not get stuck in advertising for these supplements. After all, not only do we harm, we also follow the advice below that is based on scientific research and not on current food trends.

FISHING FOR YOUR BRAIN

If you need to convince your child of the benefits of providing fish, this study can change your thinking. Scientists examined teenagers who ate fish more than once a week and found that their IQ was much higher than that of their classmates who ate fish only once a week. How do omega-3 fatty acids help your child's brain? Docosahexaenoic acid (DHA) and eicosatetraenoic acid (EPA) are polyunsaturated fatty acids in the omega-3 family. Your body cannot make these essential nutrients, so you need to get them from the food you eat. DHA is a crucial element of the brain and nervous system. The lack of omega-3 fatty acids causes various cognitive problems in childhood, including learning difficulties, poor memory, and low concentration. Scientists are discussing whether fish oil supplements can offer the same benefits. Some studies show that children who take fish oil as a dietary supplement have higher brain activity in attention-related areas than children who take a placebo. Be careful with supplements and only buy from trusted sources. If you do not want to use supplements, try serving oily fish once a week to see the benefits.

Here are some fish-like delicacies that are perfect for your child:

SALMON
Salmon is high on the list of the best fish for your brain. But it's not just salmon that does the trick. Wild salmon is much better than farmed salmon. Wild salmon is not only a good source of omega-3 fatty acids, but it is also low in mercury. Fish caught in the wild can grow, which means that their muscles and tissues are stronger.

SARDINES
Another fish is an excellent source of omega-3 fatty acids. Like salmon, sardines have low mercury content. However, be aware that canned sardines can have high cholesterol levels.

TUNA
Eating tuna has many health benefits, including canned tuna. For example, tuna is an excellent source of omega-3 fatty acids and is associated

with a reduced risk of Alzheimer's. Keep in mind that this section contains tuna, but it should remember. Canned tuna is rich in mercury and can be dangerous for pregnant women. Mercury is a toxin that can damage the baby's brain during pregnancy, and some doctors recommend pregnant women to avoid tuna altogether.

TREAT PEOPLE YOU LIKE AND PEOPLE YOU DO NOT LIKE

Inspirational children are known, especially when it comes to food. My three-year-old is no exception. Therefore, we always follow three rules when introducing new foods.

COOK WITH AN EXCITING STORY

If your boy loves to talk about pirates and dinosaurs. When we made salmon-based fish pies for the first time, we had a fantastic pirate adventure story during a meal. It worked, and now he's enjoying his explanation so much that he has a positive relationship with eating salmon. If you do not want to tell the story, go to your local library and get a book where your children can read the instructions and relate them to a new food. For example, when Sousse gave gifts to children with spinach and eggs, the mother spoke of reading classic green eggs and ham. Give your children another activity that they can enjoy when introducing new foods. If your child likes to dye, get him a new coloring book when you give him a sardine meal. When a child thinks of a fresh meal, he combines it with activities that he enjoys. So, the idea is positive.

BECOME A MODEL

If a child sees you are enjoying a fish, it is also more likely to eat it. Serve new food while eating with your family. When a child sees another person enjoying food, they are more interested in trying it. Think about how much food you want.

WAIT UNTIL YOU ARE HUNGRY

Do not give snacks or drinks (enough water) just before eating. This way, the child is more likely to enjoy every meal and try new foods. Snacks for a better brain Researchers suggest that child nutrition is the culprit of behavioral problems. A lot of research has done in this area, but most importantly, the wrong food does not cause Attention Deficit Hyperactivity Disorder (ADHD). If you are a parent and are concerned about your child's behavior at home or school, this section provides advice on how to control your child's behavior through diet.

DO NOT ADD ANY ADDITIVES

Additives are food colors and preservatives that usually found in highly processed sugar-rich foods. As you read the food label, you may see items like FD & C Yellow (E number) have the proposes to increase.

SKIP CANDY

On average, children consume about two pounds of sugar a week. The next time you go shopping, look at the size of the sugar pack. It is a tremendous amount of sugar that goes far beyond what children need. Too much sugar can lead to hyperactivity and impulsivity. Given these behaviors, we can imagine the pictures of children bouncing off the wall. But it can be much worse. A high sugar intake not only leads to destructive and aggressive behavior such as throwing and kicking but can even damage them. Younger children are most affected by the dreaded "sugar high." That's why we often eat snacks, but we leave sweets as they are. It is a snack and not a typical meal for children.

EAT GOOD FAT

Omega 3 is also ideal for children. However, your body is unable to produce these types of fatty acids. So, you have to remove them from the food. Studies show that children with low omega-3 levels are more likely to have behavioral problems like hyperactivity. Another side effect of the lack of fatty acids is an increased risk of eczema, allergies, and asthma. All of this can alleviate by boosting your child's fatty acid intake. The "Brain Fishing" section in this chapter provides tips on how to include fatty acids in your child's diet.

KNOWLEDGE IS POWER

Studies show that parent groups with little information about ADHD and the effects of diet on children are less likely to seek support and treatment. Do not wait until it's too late to give your child the help they need. As a parent, you can get the best start by making sure that your child's diet is healthy, nutritious, and does not process sugary foods.

Both fructose and glucose are the sugars your body needs. It is a form of carbohydrates that your body converts to energy. Your body uses this energy not only for physical activity but also for mental work. Low sugar levels can affect decision making and thinking. Where do you get sugar from if you need to avoid it from processed foods like candy bars? Fructose and glucose are different fructose found in some vegetables like fruits, juices, and tomatoes. Most carbohydrates (including rice, pasta, potatoes) contain glucose. At the beginning of the day, we recommend eating foods that are high in glucose. There the body can transform itself into the body and brain energy. When you eat foods that are high in glucose, your body ultimately stores them as fat instead of converting them into energy.

DEVELOPMENT OF EATING HABITS

In life, most people are probably on a diet at some point in their lives. Most people are concerned about the challenges of calorie counting, whether it's a good-looking event or a health issue. However, counting calories and switching from one diet plan to another is not the right way to live. You know that the diet plan that is likely part of your lifestyle is much more effective. This section lists foods that show that research is a critical element of every lifestyle. Do not worry. You do not have to eat like a rabbit.

HEAVY

Juice bars are everywhere these days, and nowadays it is not difficult to find even a small airport. What is so great about juice? And how can they benefit your brain? For starters, the liquid is full of vitamins. If you use juice, you can throw it together. You can try all kinds of combinations like celery and apples, cabbage and mango, broccoli and raspberries. The list is endless. You do not even need cooking skills! The following is a list of fruits that should be at the top of the juice list.

POMEGRANATE

Pomegranate juice has become popular recently. Pomegranate juice is great fun to drink, and studies confirm that unlike most food-borne illnesses, this does the hype justice. First, pomegranate is a "superfood." However, pomegranate is rich in antioxidants and more common than other fruits. Pomegranate juice characterized by pregnancy to adulthood. At the end of life, pregnant women who drink this juice can help the baby's brain to resist brain damage from hypoxia. At the other end, research has confirmed that pomegranate juice helps prevent Alzheimer's disease and maintain the health of older people.

TRIM

When pomegranate is a "trendy" fruit, people often think that plums are out of date. Most people associate plums with relief from constipation and other related bladder disorders. But do you know that plum is suitable for your brain? Plums contain vitamin A. Vitamin A not only strengthens the body's defense system but also helps the brain cells to repair themselves quickly. You can make plum juice by soaking 1 cup of plum in 5 cups of water for 4 hours. Remove the seeds, make a puree, and enjoy.

BE "ELEGANT"

Grape juice is rich in flavonoids. It lowers blood pressure and increases cholesterol. Studies have shown that grape juice can improve memory and coordination. If you already like grape juice, try drinking red or purple grape juice. These grapes packaged with excellent brain-promoting properties. A study found that grape juice is better for the heart than cranberry or orange juice.

BLUEBERRIES

Blueberries are another superfood and are rich in vitamin C and potassium (which help the bones). Clinical studies have shown that 2 cups a day is enough to improve learning and brain strength. Frozen blueberries have the same effect on the brain so that you can enjoy them all year round. You may have heard of the Atkins diet. It means that you must cut out all of the sugar (including fruit), but you can get plenty of protein and fat like steak and bacon. We do not recommend the Atkins diet (or any other diet!), But a high protein diet has advantages. When you eat protein, your brain produces a variety of chemicals, gives you energy, and stays alert, but not used much. Protein-rich foods make up only 10-15% of daily calories. Chicken and lean meat offer the best sauce. Vegetarians can fix proteins in dairy products, legumes, and nuts. As with most good things, you pay for a high protein diet. Red meat is high in cholesterol and can affect health and the brain. Scientific studies have shown that people who are rich in saturated fats and cholesterol are more likely to suffer from memory loss. Their working memory (ability to remember and manipulate information) is insufficient. How does such a diet affect your brain? This type of malnutrition causes inflammation of the brain. This inflammation affects not only memory but also physical functions such as seeing and hearing. The key is to use the right amount and limit red meat to once a week.

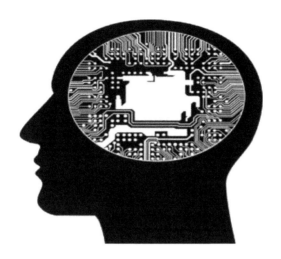

SHOW THE WAY TO SUCCESS

There is a direct connection between vocal talent and success in life. Not only do they complete crossword puzzles, unravel anagrams and understand antonyms, but all of these activities are also great for verbal use. Talk generally about the ability to use words, manipulate language, and communicate ideas, thoughts, opinions, and emotions well. Maybe politicians and lawyers make the most of this ability, as do rap artists and talk show organizers. All of them are good at attracting a broad audience with the power of words and influencing the mindset of the audience. In short, the higher your verbal intelligence, the more confident you are at enforcing your needs and desires. They are better understood and can build closer relationships. Whichever way you go, improving oral fitness can have a significant impact on social progress and prosperity.

LANGUAGE AND VISION

At the age of five, scientists believe that the vocabulary already contains about 2,000 to 3,000 words, but they do not know the exact meaning of these words. For example, a child watching a ball might say something else, but it could say "ball," which points to a balloon, chocolate egg, or pebbles. It suggests that seeing at an intuitive level has a profound impact on language development. For example, consider the first alphabetical book a child sees. Images used to decorate the letters of the alphabet and give them meaning. Not surprisingly, infants use the same words in similar shapes until the vocabulary grows, such as Apple's "A" and Bear's "B." And while you might think that this "visual" dependency increases with school attendance (a vocabulary of around 50,000 words has accumulated), analogies, metaphors, and synonyms. Consider using visual concepts affect language throughout your life. For example, speakers and powers know that using words to tell a story that reminds you of the "big picture" increases the likelihood that you will stay involved. Words may evaporate, but when you use them to convey a picture, the ideas behind them become more unforgettable. Great speakers always relied on "visual" for their fashion speech. Consider Martin Luther King's famous national address. The sentence "I have a dream ..." immediately opens a window to his vision of the future.

LANGUAGE AND INTELLIGENCE

Fluid intelligence and crystallization intelligence are common elements of intelligence. Fluid intelligence is the ability to make sense of chaos and solve new problems. Crystallized intelligence is the knowledge and skills accumulated over a lifetime and is used to perform familiar tasks. How does the language fit? Well, as a child, you will learn to use your fluid intelligence to understand your parents' language and then communicate with them. All nuances of grammar, syntax, and other languages take shape during puberty. At this point, the main areas of the brain that body new information and skills are smaller. Therefore, learning a language is much more comfortable at a young age.

DEVELOP A BILINGUAL BRAIN

Learning a new language in adulthood is not impossible. I recommend this as it is one of the best ways to activate neurons, keep your brain active, and record instruments. These activities are psychologically demanding because they force the brain to process new information and make new connections. Learning a foreign language also protects the brain from age damage. Studies show that bilingual people have fewer mental disorders due to aging than people who only speak one language.

FLOWING WORDS

Improving your vocabulary will quickly improve your intelligence. The average person speaks about 1,000 words, and more than 3 million names can give to the brain. So, there is a lot of room for improvement. The wider the vocabulary, the more it stimulates the brain by interacting with cells when speaking, reading, and writing. Public speaking can be beneficial in schools, business, and social situations. You can think more carefully about more complicated things. Verbal language skills offer the double advantage of thinking faster under pressure and speaking more calmly under pressure.

READING COMPREHENSION

Reading is an integral part of language development. The ability to understand and manipulate text can move the brain in various ways to improve perception, reason, problem-solving, and other cognitive skills. It is an essential skill that you can learn as a child, grow as a student, and apply to your career and daily life. A typical reading usually answers some questions related to a passage of text. Exercises test your ability to derive logical thinking from simple life situations.

READ EYES

Understanding requires adequate reading comprehension, depending on your ability to recognize words quickly and easily. The eye plays an important role here because it conveys information about the visual pathways. The average reading speed for Roman is 200 to 220 words/minute. Nothing interferes with your ability to decipher the meaning since you put more effort into reading individual words and sentences than trying to understand the idea expressed.

WORDS AND PICTURES

Historians follow a method of storytelling through a series of photographs of the earliest civilizations of humanity. Since then, however, art forms that combine words and images have developed. For example, until the advent of American comic book formats in the early 20th century, there were devices such as speech bubbles, flashing lightbulb symbols above the word head, bright idea symbols, and certain typographic symbols. They introduced to represent curses. The first comic book was a newspaper anthology with a humorous story about the adventures of Buck Rogers, Tarzan, Phantom, and Tinton. The late cartoonist Will Eisner called it "sequential art" rather than "comic." Over the years, many educational institutions have used comic book stories to develop oral thinking and understanding skills. We will respond more proactively to the combination of words and images. In a world where there is too much visual material, comics offer a fun and effective way to improve reading and writing. For fun exercises, you can cut the cartoon into individual cells, mix them, and put them back together. You can also combine sections to find another way to create an entirely different story.

BUILD A STORY

Storytelling is an ancient verbal art that shows the power of words to express thoughts, ideas, and emotions. We used it to spread the news, convey wisdom, and learn about the history of others and our culture. Storytelling is a widely used tool to connect people of all ages and races. It is also a powerful tool for developing and improving skills in language areas such as semantics (word meaning), syntax (word formation), and phonology (speech sounds). Storytelling uses language artistically to develop all the essential components of the communication process. Storytelling improves hearing, improves verbal expression, improves understanding, creates mental images, and stimulates oral thinking. It is the most comprehensive way to improve your oral fitness.

THE CONNECTION BETWEEN BODY AND MIND

HEALTHY BODY, STRONG MIND

Physical exercise is required to maintain the shape of the body. Nobody agrees. But how does the brain work in all of these areas? Well, the famous Latin word in ancient Roman times is "Sano Manzana of the human body," which means "healthy mind of a healthy body." It seems that the Romans were interested in something here. Sport has long known to maintain overall health and well-being.

Further research shows that activity is one of the best ways to protect your brain. If previous scientific studies did not show this, it would be surprising if it did not. Physical activity increases your heart rate, and jogging for 5 minutes at the beginning of each day also increases blood flow to your entire body, including the brain. People in their fifties who exercise regularly have better memory and concentration than people who live sedentary lives. People who continue physical activity up to the age of 60 are less likely to suffer from mental decline as some age-related cognitive impairments are due to physical inactivity and lack of mental stimulation.

WHAT ARE AEROBICS?

Physical activities such as walking, jogging, and dancing raise your heart rate to 60-80% of your maximum capacity in 15 minutes. It allows the lungs to draw more oxygen than the heart pumps through the vascular system. You should be able to speak while doing aerobic exercise. If you haven't exercised for a while, it is a good idea to have a medical exam before starting an exercise program.

PHYSICAL CHARGING

Maintaining energy levels throughout the day is difficult. At some point, you may feel tired or feel that your brain is no longer able to think clearly. When many people are sick, they drink coffee or take a bar of chocolate and use caffeine and sugar spikes to restore energy levels. However, this is an unhealthy and short-term solution. Another way to increase energy is to move the body for a few minutes. It improves blood circulation and immediately increases attention.

STRESSOR

Stress arises when a person feels overwhelmed by the pressure of life and cannot handle it. The keyword here is "feel." Stress weakens creativity, and memory because priorities are recognizing mental demands that affect physical well-being. Focus is not necessarily a bad thing. You need to reach a moderate level to stay focused and stimulated. However, if the stress is too high and out of control, the effects are counterproductive and can affect health. A chemical called glutamate gets into the brain and can be harmful. People are fed up with too many demands, lose confidence, and are ultimately frustrated. It can lead to forgetfulness, misplaced things, misunderstandings in conversation, snapshots with others, etc. Excessive stress makes both the brain and the body inefficient.

BUSTER FOR PHYSICAL EXERCISE

If you find that most reviews are in the very tense fields, you need to find a way to adjust your stress level. Many people use a common technique called Progressive Muscle Relaxation (PMR). PMR is about exaggerating tensions to promote calm and body. Tense every muscle group in your body until it hurts (about 20 seconds) and then release it. Blood flows into this area, creates warm feelings, relieves tension, and soothes. PMRs also act as sleeping pills.

GO EAST

For thousands of years, people in the Orient have been using various techniques to seek harmony between mind, body, and soul. Western medicine is traditionally skeptical of oriental therapies such as Zen, Tai Chi, and Yoga. However, increasing evidence, especially from scientific studies using brain scanning techniques, has shown that ancient Eastern Buddhists lower blood pressure and breathe. It shows that you know how to slow down, release muscle tension, and organize your mind. In today's fast-paced world, people are under more significant pressure. The body responds typically by releasing stress response hormones like cortisol. It circulates the system and incorrectly blocks the formation of new neurons in the hippocampus. We now know that all types of meditation exercises help the body regulate stress hormone levels.

ZAZEN

Zen meditation is a practice that is at the center of Zen's belief. The goal is to focus your mind, sometimes with mantras, sounds, or breathing, to promote a completely calm state. The meditator sits quietly, pays attention to simple songs, and sorts out all the antiques in his head, such as negative thoughts, and feelings. This state of mind often referred to as "mindfulness." In the West, about 10 million people practice meditation every day. There are different techniques, but the primary purpose is to recognize the flow of thoughts, generate ideas, and die without interruption. Empirical data suggests that Zen meditation relieves depression symptoms and improves sleep quality.

MEDITATE

Whether you are sitting or standing, it is essential that you keep your back straight and in the right position. The goal is to get rid of all distractions and achieve a "heartless" state. To achieve this, you need to pay attention to the sensory experience, not your sense of it. For example, if you suddenly hear the noise, do not think about it, just listen. When entering meditation, the EEG pattern should shift from the right frontal cortex to the gentle left frontal cortex. It reduces the adverse effects of stress, mild depression, and anxiety.

ACUPUNCTURE AND BRAIN

Acupuncture is an ancient Chinese cure for many diseases, in which practitioners insert thin needles into defined points on the patient's body from which the life energy "Ki" flows. There are more than 1,500 "points" on the whole body. Acupuncture works by inactivating or "calming" critical areas of the brain and is used to relieve acute mood disorders, pain, and food cravings. The science behind it is not yet understood, and clinical studies on acupuncture are still inconclusive. However, several studies in volunteers monitored with fMRI brain scans have shown that within a few seconds of receiving acupuncture, blood flow in some regions of the brain reduced. Other studies have found that acupuncture helps treat depression, eating disorders, addiction, and pain. However, critics believe that positive results are likely the result of a placebo effect. There is general agreement that acupuncture is safe when administered by a qualified doctor using sterile needles. However, many doctors generally reject the treatment because the idea of "Qi" and its various pathways is incompatible with modern biomedical knowledge.

YOGA
Yoga is an ancient custom that started in India and has existed for over 5,000 years. Like Thai Chi, it combines breathing exercises with postures and meditation. Although tai chi is classified as a gentle martial art and requires energy to focus on the elegance of the workout, yoga is similar to traditional body training. It is maintaining a particular posture and control of breathing. Yoga is said to calm the nervous system and balance body and mind. Some practitioners claim that yoga can keep specific energy paths open and give life energy to prevent certain illnesses. Yoga is becoming increasingly popular around the world. Yoga has been used to lower blood pressure, relieve stress, improve coordination, flexibility, focus, sleep, and digestion. In one study, regular yoga exercises increased Gamma-Aminobutyric Acid (GABA) levels in the brain. This amino acid plays a crucial role in regulating neuronal excitability throughout the nervous system. It is advisable to look for yoga as a possible treatment for depression and anxiety disorders associated with low GABA levels.

SLEEP AND BRAIN

Nothing is refreshing enough to sleep soundly. We feel ready to get up and face the challenges of the day. It is because the growth hormone is released during sleep and heals damaged tissue, including brain tissue. Sleep also helps lubricate the gears of the cognitive system and transfer information to long-term memory by "reviewing and remembering" the day's experience. Sleep regulates a body clock known as the "circadian rhythm." The body clock is, of course, recorded by the eye in sync with the daily cycle of light and dark. For this reason, jet lag occurs after a long flight, and it takes a while for the body clock to reset.

HOW MUCH SLEEP?

The amount of sleep you need depends on the person. Some people spend 5 hours a night, while others take 9 hours. It is essential to know what your "magic number" is and to stick to that number. Otherwise, you risk losing productivity and being less able to remember and process information. Lack of sleep puts a massive strain on the brain. Studies have shown that sleepless minds lose efficiency. Other parts of the brain must support areas that are usually active during specific tasks. It is like driving a vehicle with flat tires, which results in significantly reduced performance. Deprivation of sleep also increases the level of stress hormones and reduces the production of nerve cells (neurogenesis) in the adult brain.

PHASES OF SLEEP

Sleep is divided into separate brain stages. There are theta waves that occasionally squeak with sudden movements. Next, there is a triangular wave activity. In the meantime, you completely lose your sense of direction when you wake up. While sleeping, these two EEG patterns alternate in a 90-minute cycle. Then go to REM sleep, where the eyelids appear to be on alert.

NEW HABITS TO TRAIN THE BRAIN

You can quickly enter the rut and repeat the same thing every day. Well, today is the day to make changes. The idea that learning something new is a great way to keep your brain sharp has scientific reasons. The hippocampus guarantees that new neurons created every day to support learning and memory. When you learn something new, these neurons can stay alive and slow your cognitive decline. This chapter presents some ideas you can use to start keeping your brain healthy and sharp.

TRY LINE DANCE

If you think line dance reserved for a dusty bar full of smoke swirls and cowboy boots, think again. Line dancing not only keeps you healthy, but it also increases your serotonin level and makes your brain more comfortable. As the name suggests, line dance is a place where a series of steps take place in a room. Line dance is not as easy as it looks, but it is fun. And you can choose from many different routines and steps. Keeping the brain active is difficult when you learn new steps. Grab a partner and go to the next salon! Optional cowboy boots.

Here are some dance tips to get you started:

DO NOT LOOK AT YOUR FEET

Line dance is useful when you look up to the teacher or the DVD. If you look up, you can gather information about body and leg movements. A look down can distract you if your legs do not move as expected. Raise your eyes and move your legs!

LEARN THE PROCEDURE

Remembering is a great way to train your brain. It encourages the brain to learn new things and dedicate them to long-term memory. If you do not have to worry about the next level of the dance routine, you can enjoy the experience even more.

THINK AHEAD

Predict the next step in the routine. Close your eyes and think about what your feet should do next. In this way, the brain trained not only to keep track of what others were doing but also to remember a series of dance sequences.

PUZZLE

Puzzles are not just for children. Creating puzzles is a great way to improve collaboration and spatial thinking. If you haven't done a puzzle in a while and you feel like you can't start, choose a mystery to get started. Do not try the 1,000-piece landscape puzzle. Let's start with the secret of your favorite animal. It can be a favorite animal or a well-known painting. This way, you can use the knowledge of the image in your head to solve the puzzle.

BEFORE YOU START THE PUZZLE, DO THE FOLLOWING:

1. Before you begin the puzzle, you must first make sure that all the pieces are facing up. It may take a little longer, but the puzzle time becomes much quieter and, therefore, fun. And if you have a good time, you are more likely to continue the puzzle. You can also stack them in batches with the pieces facing up or create different piles with puzzle corners and edges.

2. Go to the border. The next step is to build the wall. It's relatively easy, but "miracle" gets a lot easier. If you can't find all the edge pieces, make sure they're not too long. It circulates in an open room.

3. Then start working on the mountain. Start with the simplest. Some people find it best to start with a large object in the puzzle. Others think that color classification is a good starting point because they are so diverse and easy to combine. Do not be frustrated. Do not forget to start with a simple puzzle. You do not want to face such a difficult challenge that you can't even solve the first puzzle.

LEARN A LANGUAGE

There are many cheap airlines out there, so it was not easy to take a short weekend trip. And is there no better excuse to learn the language than ordering Italian ice cream on a hot day or looking for the essentials in an exotic place in the market? Not only are you happy to feel like a local during your vacation, learning a language can bring considerable benefits to your brain. Brain scans show that some bilingual people in mind have dark gray matter associated with their visual-spatial abilities (parietal cortex).

Language learning has become even more convenient, with so many digital resources. You can learn in less than 10 minutes a day, from a range of for Dummies titles (using the iPhone app for language learning) to free online sound clips with common phrases in different languages of interest. Recommended new words and sentences.

It helps you know that you can use new skills. So, think of the language you want to switch to immediately. If you'd like to stay here instead, here are some suggestions on how to practice your language skills at home.

FIND FRIENDS

Develop friendships with other language learners and native speakers. Then speak and plan only in that language. It may be difficult to talk at first, but learning the language itself is much faster. Choose a place like a cafe or a restaurant so you can practice writing before you meet.

READ A BOOK

Most local libraries have books in the language that came with the CD. If you do not want to invest in a language programmer, we recommend a local library. A great way to practice your language is to look for children's books written in the language you are learning.

SING A SONG

Songs are a fun and catchy way to learn new sentences. With rhythm, lyrics, and buzz, you can quickly learn new things. Increase the volume. Who knows, maybe you'll discover a sentence or two to make your vacation more romantic.

GO TO NEW PARK

Changing the scene can make a big difference in mental health. No significant changes required, e.g., Moving to a new city. But small changes can make a big difference. For example, if you bring a dog that runs in the same place every day, change the route today! You may not notice it, but seeing the same trees and flowers every day can be distracting. It is easy to find new places to enjoy. You will be amazed at how energetic you are when you can look into your new surroundings. Refresh your mood when you return from vacation. My eyes are bright, my worries are gone, and everything in the world is right and wonderful. You can restore the experience a bit by changing the physical environment. If you are usually on foot or by bike, change the route frequently. If you can stop working early in the morning, you will be back on a more extended, picturesque road home. Enjoy the chirping of the birds and the blooming of the flowers. Think about the beautiful things you will see on your trip.

EAT NEW FOOD

Sharing experiences with friends is always more fun. So, if you do not try a new meal yourself, invite friends. Encourage your friends to try something new.
In this way, you can strengthen your brain and enjoy the benefits of foods that enjoy each

other's company. The entire menu does not have to consist of new food. Try a new one once a month.

JOIN THE BOOK CLUB

The Book Club is a great way to regenerate your mental muscles. Reading is a great activity, but it's even better to share what you are reading with a group of friends. Book clubs are a great way to share ideas and discover new things. If you do not have a book club near you, get started. Here are some tips to get you started.

FIND THE TIME

The first thing to do is to choose the best time for you and your friends. For example, if you need to take your child to school to meet. Or if you are in a hurry to work, nights are probably the best time. It is essential that you do not view the book club as a chore or additional activity, but rather that you can relax part of your schedule.

THINK OF NIBBLES

Everything seems to have improved with snacks! When you host a book club, you do not have to be a slave in the kitchen for hours. Simple things like vegetables or dips are fine. You can rotate them and bring them one after the other. It not only relieves your pressure but also ensures that everyone can bite something while you are discussing the book.

SELECT A BOOK

The most important part of the book club is, of course books! Please choose a different genre for each month. You can start with a detective story for a month and then switch to another genre the next month. It can be a popular science book. You can also choose the fiction bestseller first. Often the bestsellers are included in the film, so you can think about your plans before you start reading the book.

WRITE A FILM REVIEW

Think about what you like and what you do not like in this film and write about 100 words to explain your thoughts. Think carefully about why you focused on an aspect of the film. You must come up with one or two ideas. Movies are more comfortable to speak.

SAVE THE SCREAM

Doing what is logical in reviews is more beneficial to you than being emotional. Do not shout at reviews. Instead, carefully review the discussion for a review. If possible, do not generalize the view. Discuss this in as much detail as possible.

Focus on one scene and use it as an example of what you like or dislike in a movie.

BECOME AN ENTHUSIASTIC FILM FAN

Explain how a film improves or deteriorates by comparing it to another movie. Anchors help develop ideas. By comparing the two, the brain can combine different images. As a result, you will find that you can improve your daily conversation.

LET US PUBLISH!

Spend 5 minutes every morning. Mental health is essential for brain function. So, make sure your problem doesn't overwhelm you. Calm down, meditate, and find the moment every morning to prepare for the day. You may need to wake up a little earlier so you can escape the morning madness in your home. But it's worth it. Perhaps you have a cup of coffee or tea ready for the day. Or maybe you just want to sit and enjoy the silence.

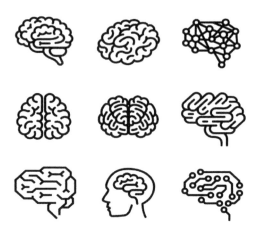

CUSTOMIZE THIS FACE

The next time you are looking for a recognizable face in a newspaper or magazine, list three things you can remember about that person. A person can be a politician, actor, or singer. No matter who he is, try to find out what facts you know about him. You can also do it with your friends. Check out the school yearbook and old photo albums. It's a great time to move your brain and remember not only a person's name but also the facts about that person. It could be something like sitting next to him in chemistry class or changing a joke in music class. Above all, practice these connections, prevent weakening, and keep your brain active.

FIND AN OBJECT

This game is perfect for visiting new places. If you are waiting in the clinic or café, try this game. Look around the room for 1 minute. Close your eyes and think of 10 things you saw in the room. It takes 10 seconds to create these objects. Please note down as much as you can remember. For example, if you have a magazine on the table, do not just of magazine. Think of a magazine title. What was on the cover, are there any main keywords? How about the plants? Did you see it in the room? Think as detailed as possible. Would you like to try more? Try this. Give only 10 seconds to remember 20 in the place. Here too, you name not only the object but also remember its function.

TOP GAMES

Please choose a category. Let's say its food. Set a time limit. 1 minute? Name as many foods as you can in a minute. How was it? Most people can list about 30 foods. Push yourself to hit that number. Buy 60 items. Here is another way to make this difficult. Choose a category and a time limit. Then select the letter. Say the letter D. Within 30 seconds after the letter D, name as many foods as possible. You can exchange "race" words with your friends to see who can name more food. Remember to pay attention to the timer. An essential part of this training game is to find as many objects as possible in a short time. It trains your brain to think faster.

NUMBERS GAME

Start with a high number like 100 and countback with 2. That count is 100, 98, 96, 94, and so on. It will be easy. Count down 3 or 4 and challenge. If you want to challenge yourself, set a time limit. Or try another method to make it even more difficult.

MEMORY GAME

This game is called the N-Back task, and you must save it in the order you saw it. Psychologists have found that people who have been trained in these activities three times a week for 20 weeks have improved IQ and memory. It is your job. Ask a friend to read the next letter. Every time you look at the bold letters, you will ask if you heard the same name three letters before.

X C E B S E I X OS X P O W E Q W X K H K (etc.)

For example, the answer to E is yes. For the letter S, the answer is no. You can also do this activity with shapes and photos. Is it too easy? Try the same action. Do it now while singing your favorite song. It's too easy to try the same activity but look at the same letter (or figure or photo), three letters (or model or image) to see if you sang your favorite song. Can you help your friends? Would you like to try this game by car on the street? Think about the color of the vehicle. Then ask yourself: "Are there two red cars?" It is more complicated than we expected!

PLEASE TELL ME THE STORY

If you get bored and wait at the train station or airport, this is the perfect game. Find someone who looks interesting. Now think about the story for that person. Why is he there? What is the reason for his trip? The goal of this activity is to be creative. Imagine that you are a novelist, and that person is the character in your story. Create his motive, the reason for his actions. Think about what will happen next in the story. Be as creative as you want. After all, this is your story. Read Chapter 8 for more information on the benefits of the creative mind.

DRUMS FOR YOUR BRAIN

I need a friend to help me with this, but it's a great activity while I'm waiting. Ask a friend to sing a song in his head. But he can't tell you what the subject is. Next, ask about the rhythm of the music you play at the table. Listen carefully and tap the rhythm once your friends complete. Try to remember the rhythm. Make the beat as accurate as possible—rhythm memory, which is closely related to speech memory. You will also improve your language skills by training how well you can master a certain rhythm.

READ A CHALLENGING BOOK

It doesn't just read the usual newspapers and magazines that make you happy. Would you like to try something new? Usually, when reading fiction, you choose a historical novel instead. Reading new things is a great way to broaden your horizons and think about your brain in new ways.

FUN TO SHOOT

If you can't let go of the daily newspaper, you'll find newspaper and magazine activities here. Hold down the stylus and set the clock for this activity. Proceed as follows:

1. Set a time limit. Start from 10 seconds.

2. Select a word.

3. Within 10 seconds, take the pen and round off the dozens on the side.

The game is perfect for visual training, learning how to find visual clues quickly, and training the speed of your brain.

HURRY-UP

Choose from crossword puzzles, word puzzles, logic games, and Sudoku for simple, complicated, or dangerous options. Chapters have something for everyone and make your brain work.

SCRAMBLE WORD

Some people love crossword puzzles, logical puzzles, word searches, word encryption, and other word playable puzzles. They seem to have the trick to solve them. Others are talentless and do not recognize it when they hit their foreheads. How do you get the hang of it? What if you wanted to say, "Do not wake me up tonight!" From the front of the puzzle (other than having the answer at hand)? Many start puzzles at school and teachers hire students to solve puzzles and improve spelling, reading, science, or other lessons. You may have known the structure of most of these puzzles for a long time and have probably experienced them at least.

But that doesn't mean we're satisfied. You can be very nervous today when you play crossword puzzles. What is a better way to test the amount of knowledge that we have collected and stored over the years? And what could be nicer than staring at a hint and feeling more like a full dipstick? And maybe you are ready to overcome fear. It's still fun after overcoming fear and frustration.

Word scramble puzzles can play in different ways. Look at a group of letters arranged in a random order, use all the letters, and rearrange them into words. Sorted words are only 5-8 characters long. To solve this puzzle, for example, decipher the capital letters. Where the sauce gets darker: _ _ _ _ _ _ _ By the way, the answer to this puzzle is the kitchen. Decoding words of this length is usually not very difficult. The difficulty increases with the increasing number of letters and words. Try to solve this, for example: Where is the best place to meet the headmaster? _ _ _ _ _ _ _ _ _ _

The answer is the classroom. The strategy against word encryption is simple.

• If you are dealing with a series of swear words, check them one by one to ensure that they do not pop out. You will be amazed at how quickly some problems can be solved. The mind seems to have made it for this kind of work.

• If you do not see the answer, write the letters in a different order. Do not worry if you write a sentence right away. Merely rearranging the letters in a new order can cause the moment you watch.

• It is still confusing but tries to group the characters logically. Consider the number of vowels. If there are twice as many consonants as vowels, the word can start with a consonant. Sort the letters until you find what you are looking for. You can also randomly arrange the letters in a circle to change the appearance of the letters. Eventually, you will come across a brilliant combination.

For example, when you write down a player, you must write down the game, the rays, and the levels. You can write salaries, years, etc., but most importantly, carefully arrange your words in the long-term order you create. These are the easiest ways.

CONCLUSION

I hope the information provided in this book will help with your Brain Training. It will help you in learning and will make you perform co-curricular activities more effectively. It will improve your memory. Different methods and experiences will help in your Brain Training. We want to keep the body active, but why not keep an eye on the same amount of care? Everyone is told to go to the gym and exercise to stay healthy, but somehow the same need for our brain health isn't given. We may think that just reading or studying here is enough, but research shows that changes in our mental activity are key to long-term success.

Intelligence is not just a fixed function with which you were born. Here at Neuro-Nation, we strive to keep our brains busy, so we can maximize our potential. Whether you want to improve your memory, be more intelligent, or have a better attention span - we're here to help you. Try it out and start training today.

COPYRIGHTS

© Copyright 2020 By James Goodchild All rights reserved

This book

the written permission of the publisher and all liberties authorized.

The information provided here is correct and reliable, as any lack of attention or other means resulting from the misuse or use of the procedures or instructions contained therein is the total and absolute obligation of the user addressed.

The author is not obliged, directly or indirectly, to assume civil liability for any restoration, damage, or loss resulting from the data collected here. The respective authors retain all copyrights not kept by the publisher.

The information contained herein is solely and universally available for information purposes. The data is presented without a warranty or promise of any kind.

The trademarks used are without approval, and the patent is issued without the trademark owner's permission or protection.

The logos and labels in this book are the property of the owners themselves and are not associated with this text.

Lightning Source UK Ltd.
Milton Keynes UK
UKHW020703270223
417728UK00015B/1273